Patri

God Bless
Pat

God in my Life

How God Speaks to Me

God In My Life - How God Speaks to Me

Copyright 2015 by Patricia Schiissler

Illustrations by Sharla Webster

Tellwell Talent

www.tellwell.ca

ISBN
Softcover: 978-1-988186-75-7
Hardcover: 978-1-988186-76-4
eBook: 978-1-988186-74-0

"I started talking to God when I was little but never expected Him to start talking back to me."

TABLE OF CONTENTS

CHAPTER 1:

how it all began

Somewhere deep inside me, there has always been a desire to write a book. Every time that I encountered a new spiritual experience, I would suppress an urge to begin writing about it and its affect on my life. Excuses would be made about the time commitment being an issue. A desire also existed to become a teacher. Memories related by my parents, tell of lining up dining room chairs in a row and trying to teach my grandmother. Of course, I was the teacher and grandmother was the student. My third, major desire was to be a participant of some form in the celebration of the Mass. I had a paralyzing fear of speaking in front of people and never thought I would be capable of something like that. Most people of the church, and especially women were not admitted into the sanctuary during my early years. These wishes aren't something that can be explained, they just are, and have existed within as God created me.

I was born and raised on a small, mixed farm near Melville, Saskatchewan, Canada. It was only six miles from town but for my father it might as well have been a hundred miles. Our family never ventured too far from home unless it was really necessary. Thanks to this endless, minimally eventful time, my imagination and creativity evolved. I preferred my self-created world and would spend hours and hours in personal bliss and glory. I had many pretend friends who came to visit. They were always welcome and I loved them all.

Let me introduce myself. My name is Patricia Anne Theresa (Hanowski) Schiissler. The Patricia was chosen by my father. He was in the army during the Second World War and was impacted by Princess Patricia's Light Infantry. The Anne is my beautiful mother's first name. Theresa is my confirmation name. I wanted that particular name because it belonged to my grandmother on my dad's side. Later in life, it became the female form of my husband, Terry's name. Plus, my best friend for two decades was named Terrie and I finished my teaching career at St. Theresa elementary school. It is uncanny how some names keep repeating in our lives.

My immediate family was a quite strict and devoted Roman Catholic family. Both of my parents would be called cradle Catholics. This means that they were born and baptized to practicing Roman Catholic parents. Yes, the Catholic faith is rooted back in my family for many generations, I believe. My three sisters and I were immediately baptized Roman Catholic at birth. In fact, I was baptized at St. Peter's hospital in Melville before leaving for the farm. At that time, infant death was not uncommon, though I never did know of any babies dying in our neighbourhood.

The farm house that we occupied was quite small by today's standards. It was around five hundred and some square feet on the main floor. There was an upstairs with two bedrooms. You could reach it by ascending a steep staircase that looked almost like an enhanced step-ladder. We did not have electricity so kerosene lamps were used for light. We had a wood stove in the kitchen and a small furnace in the living room. Wood was hauled into a large box located in the porch. Every evening I would go to the wood pile, a distance from the house itself and pile my arms high with the wood chunks to be burned. That chore was my responsibility, ongoing. Water was hauled in two barrels from the well by my father for drinking and washing. We did not have running water or any form of cistern until much later. We were expected to do daily chores which did teach us cooperation and responsibility. Like any child, I tried to sneak away from doing them until late in the day and instead, I would find a quiet spot to read for hours.

Reading materials were limited. I would attempt to read any book that crossed my path. Most books or old magazines were browsed over repeatedly. One magazine that remains embedded in my memory had pictures of a Royal Canadian Mounted Police graduation with all the beautiful gowns, pomp and ceremony. I spent hours staring at the gorgeous illustrations and dreaming of what could possibly become my future, but I believed never would. At that time, I could have never known that a handsome recruit from Alberta would actually invite me to escort him to such an event. It was an amazing day that I will never forget. The morning started with my escort, Gregg, demonstrating scuba diving and rescue. There was an official receiving line with police dignitaries before lunch and precision drill demonstrations. The evening finished with a banquet and dance. It was a Cinderella evening that would never be forgotten. Unfortunately, the next day, I was told during the sad parting, that Gregg was leaving for good. He had been engaged to someone and was still much in love with that person, even though she had broken it off with him. With a chin up, and a warm kiss, I knew that it was good-bye forever. Anyway, it was quite strange how the childhood dream turned into a future reality.

We had a neighbour family a couple of miles down the road who were not Catholic. The family of four, with a son and daughter near to my age, were Evangelical Brethren in faith. Seeing as I had read mostly everything at our farm house, when opportunity presented itself, I visited these neighbours and their reading materials. They had an awesome set of children's Bible Stories. Mom was critical when I would bring one of these books home because she feared our neighbours were trying to convert her children. The stories were probably not even related to a specific religion and I read them anyway.

I loved the beautiful, colour illustrations in the Bible stories. The text was also very simple to read and understand. One of my favourite parts was reading how Elijah was so lucky to be able to walk and talk with God. I really wanted to do that as well. Could you imagine the beauty of such an encounter? Being so proficient at pretending, I would often go on such walks. Common sense told me that I was entirely alone and I believed that, but as an adult, I now feel that God actually was walking and talking with me too. How could He resist all that innocent affection?

So overall, our family life was pretty blessed and happy. We had two loving parents and never lacked for food and clothing. My mother, Anne, was a great cook and prided herself on having a thriving garden. My father, William, raised livestock so we had a variety of meats. To other people, it would be just an ordinary old place with most buildings in need of paint. There were usually two or three dogs roaming around and plenty of cats. I was constantly surrounded by animal love. To me as a child, it was the best place ever. All physical aspects of life were taken care of, as well as the religious needs. Emotions were treated differently, they were not to be mentioned, or addressed without threats of a spanking. It was important to show inner strength because nobody could ever help you with what could not be seen. We were taught to handle our own problems in the best way possible within our knowledge range. We knew that we were loved by our parents, yet it was never really shown in a physical sense. There were no hugs. There was no pat on the shoulder or back for something well done. Birthdays were not generally celebrated, nor were accomplishments at school.

Dad and I would listen to Saturday night hockey games on the radio when I was little. We would cheer for Gordie Howe and the Detroit Red Wings. I also knew that Sid Abel was originally from Melville. Dad would allow me to sit on his lap, massage his scalp with my fingers and comb his hair. Being with my father was always very special to me. My loving moments always revolved around time spent with my father. He would take time to talk to me and show me things in nature, how to fix things, and what his life was like when he was growing up. I was a real dad's girl.

Unfortunately, nothing is ever pure bliss. My two older sisters loved to cause fights with me. They had a younger sister to pick on and took full advantage of it. That is mainly why I loved my own time alone, to hide, and live in my own world. My oldest sister wanted to be the best due to the default of age. She did have the edge on mom's affection. Sharryl resembled mom in appearance. She had eyes that were a brown-green colour and dark, brown hair. Her personality was more like my father, with a tendency to stagnate with jobs that should have more immediate attention. Most of her time was spent in the house, so she had the time connect with mom. She never really stressed over not completing high school. Marriage and family were priorities in her life.

My next oldest sister, Geri, (or Geraldine, as she hated to be called), was given attention for being beautiful and athletic. Admittedly, she did have soft, blond hair and bluish-green eyes. She resembled my father in appearance, with a tall, slender build. Geri had great ability for education but it never seemed to be a priority for her. She was very active and seemed to be the one in trouble with mom and dad most of the time. She was always trying something new and never was too concerned about failure. We were three girls, two years apart in age. My youngest sister, Susan, was seven years younger than me. I never really did too much with her because I hated babysitting and she was the baby of the family. Plus, she took my place as being the youngest and everybody loved to let me know about it all the time.

Call it self-pity, but I felt neither beautiful nor any sort of favourite. I always detested any type of favouritism throughout my life. My picture showed a young lady with a turned eye, wearing horrible glasses. Glasses were not stylish in that time and I usually had one of the lenses frost-coated. I also had one ear that seemed to stick out further than it should. When I had my children, their ears were adamantly and neatly pinned back. My teeth never lined up properly and I got the bowl-over-the-head haircut. Plus, I was told that I had big lips and given the nick-name of "Liver-lips". I certainly didn't portray attitude and arrogance from my reflection. Hand-made, meaning sewn by mom, and often handed-down clothes can be added to this picture as well. It is difficult to match any style with a limited selection. Red and pink together often had to do for the day. I guess you could say that I was a nerd.

The above description may partly explain why I loved my own imaginary world. My favourite spot was behind two old wooden grana-ries side-by-side, tucked away, and mostly hidden in the furthest corner of the yard. They were situated just in front of a slough with lots of trees to create shade. A barbed-wire fence ran the length of this area, with calves' generally roaming and eating grass. I spent most of my hours in this spot letting my creative energy roam free. We had limited toys to play with but I never remember being bored. I had a pretend house with all the necessary kitchen utensils consisting of old tin cans and discarded ketchup bottles, etc. My fancy mud creations were used to entertain any friends that happened to visit. Of course, they were pretend friends.

I remember a special event during one winter. It had been a mild day. I had been enjoying the outdoors, like I spent most of my waking hours. Towards evening, the sun was beginning to set. It was also starting to feel colder. If you recall, we had limited resources. As a four-year-old, I treasured all my warm winter apparel. There would not be replacements for items gone missing. I realized that while I was playing and building snow creatures, my mittens had been set on the snow somewhere. One was missing. I searched everywhere that I had played that day. There was no way that I could go in the house without that missing mitten. I began to get cold as it continued to grow dark. Time passed. I was feeling more and more desperate and decided to pray to God for help. More time passed. Finally, I promised God that if my mitten showed up, I would give Him all my love, forever. There it was. I made a slight turn from where I was crouched and the lost mitten was there, waiting to be picked up. That special, close to God moment, stayed with me all my life. It was the time that I had promised my self to God.

I feel that God was always present caring for us in our farm home. There were endless dangers. Coal oil lamps were left in our care as little children, even on nights when we were at home alone and told not to get out of bed. My parents would sometimes visit the neighbours or go to the movies and leave us alone in the house. The stove ran on wood as fuel and we used flammable kerosene to light it, when it needed restarting. We were supposed to add split wood to the stove and forgot to do so frequently. The stove would die out and be cold. We would restart the fire before our parents came in from their chores. Fires would start quickly if gas was poured on top of the paper and kindling. What a blessing that it never exploded! Even with all the dangers present, death never visited our farm. I remember jumping off shed roofs, climbing on piles of bales stacked high, and throwing sharp knives into the barn door. Thank God nobody ever opened the door and walked in at that moment. We did so many mischievous things!

My sisters and I loved when the neighbour families came to visit because we got to socialize with a large, mixed group both male and female. Playing games outdoors was the best occupation of our time. The games were simple and didn't need special equipment. We played tag, or anti-i-over where we threw the ball over the house and ran to the opposite side before being tagged. We played stealing sticks and tried to end up with the biggest pile, stolen from the opposite team. At that age we didn't think of whether we liked somebody, or if they were allowed to play. It didn't matter who was the captain. Age and speed were usually the reasons why someone was chosen. I remember playing the games without fights because we were so happy to have the company.

There are a couple of scary events ingrained in my memory from when I felt God's protection. The first one occurred when I was very young. I was probably about three or four years old. It was autumn and a very beautiful, sunny day. We had an empty granary in the yard which dad planned on moving the next day for harvest. I made myself at home in it and moved in with my paper doll family. While absorbed in my playing, I heard shouting. My parents wanted me to remain in the protection of the grain bin. The danger was from our large bull that had escaped the fence and was running around loose in the yard. Not understanding the problem, I came out of the granary and stood along the side wall. The bull charged directly to where I was standing. Just as it came mere inches from me, it stopped. It froze and stared at me. I froze and stared at it. Like a miracle, it turned and walked away. My parents were very relieved. They captured the animal immediately.

A second, scary memory is from a day when I was older, about ten years of age. Once again, it was harvest time. I had been riding my two-wheel bicycle to deliver a message to my father, who was busy working in the field. I was in a hurry to get home and didn't pay attention as I arrived in the yard. The sling rope was hanging from the top of the barn, across the path that I was using. The huge rope was used to haul the hay up into the hayloft and was very large and thick. I raced into the rope at full speed and it caught me around the neck. I went tumbling off my bike and had trouble catching my breath. I hurried to the house. My neck had huge welts and red scabs for weeks later. I was teased by my sisters that I was trying to hang myself. My parents didn't bother taking me for an examination at the hospital or doctor's office because they assumed my neck wasn't damaged. Simple accidents and occurrences were taken for granted as part of daily life. Once again, God's hand, or my Guardian angel, saved me from having a broken neck.

Sunday Mass was attended weekly. Unfortunately for us children, it was spoken in Latin and we didn't understand the words. It wasn't joyous to be in church because we were expected to sit like little statues. Mass seemed very long and usually hot in the summer, especially when we went to what was called a High Mass. This Mass was even longer than the rest. Bathroom needs were never heard of until we returned home to the farm. It seemed exceptionally long when dad would visit with his brothers after church. They would talk about their farming concerns while we stood outside and fidgeted forever. Finally it would be time to leave. Ice cream after church was used as a bribe for good behaviour and it usually worked. Misbehaviour meant going straight back to the farm in a silent car.

Real church wasn't as much fun as playing church. When alone upstairs in my room, I would put on a shawl, or a towel, create a small altar from a cardboard box with a dresser scarf and a crucifix on it, and I would be the priest. The best part was processing in at the very beginning of the Mass. I practiced that multiple times until my idea of perfection had been achieved. I loved to play Mass. I learned nearly all the Mass parts from repeating them so many times from my child's prayer book. As an adult, when I am proclaiming and am part of the procession, needless to say, the childhood memory returns. I can't help but smile when I remember practicing.

Sunday afternoons, dad would attempt to read the Bible to his children. Dad's parents used to do that when he was young. We refused to listen to him by fidgeting or complaining. Dad would then tell us to go and do other things. We thought that dad was boring. Dad was always patient with us and didn't want to force the issue. He loved to smile at everybody and be kind to them. I only remember a couple of times that he used strict discipline with us. Many years later, I finally picked up the Bible and read it from cover to cover. A couple of times, I mentioned my new reading challenge to others and was encouraged to use a special format to hold my interest. I am a cover to cover book reader and that was how I would undertake my new initiative. If I felt that I had skipped or missed something, I would need to return and see it completed. I am not quite sure why the desire became so strong to do this. But, I am glad that I read it all.

Education was always important to my parents. I began school in grade one at a one-room country school consisting of eight grades and one teacher. I was a bright student and enjoyed learning. My worst difficulty was having the confidence to speak in front of other people. It wasn't bad when we could stand beside our desks, but I didn't like speaking from the front of the classroom. At the Christmas concert, when I was given a poem to recite, I would become ill with nervous tension. By some magic, I managed to perform my assigned lines. I was so very afraid and nervous about public speaking that it haunted me most of my life. I would always wonder if I was capable of becoming a teacher due to this fear. Religion as a subject was not part of the curriculum. The priest from Killaly drove out a couple of times to teach the Catholic children some religion after regular school hours. The deserted teacher's house was available for the lessons but was very cold. We could see our breath while receiving instruction. During summer vacation, dad drove us into Melville for catechism. The classes lasted the whole day and continued for a couple of weeks. We didn't mind because occasionally we could sneak out to purchase some ice cream from the store.

One teacher had a disappointing impact on my life. I still struggle with her way of working with children even though, I have forgiven her. She probably didn't know any different way of dealing with the situation. The students were expected to memorize answers to given questions from a catechism book. I had a great memory and excelled at this activity. When the final day of classes arrived, this teacher had prizes for the top grades. She started with the third highest mark, and gave them a prize of a special bookmark. She moved on to second place and gave them a rosary. I knew that I had the top mark and was very excited. What I didn't know, was that another student, two years older than me, had the same top mark. The teacher felt that it was fair to flip a coin for the top prize of a beautifully framed picture of the Holy Family. The other student, Betty, had first choice, picked the correct coin side, and took the prize. I never had a chance, or a say in the matter, and walked away with nothing. So much for hard work and caring! I spent the rest of the afternoon trying not to cry. I didn't allow the tears to come, but it sure hurt inside. I learned to hate religion school. It also took years to forgive the other girl who won, even though it wasn't her fault. What would I have done if the winner was me? The teacher should have had two first prizes. Oh well! Just call it a learning experience.

As I progressed to grade four, my parents learned that teachers at the farm school were being requested to fail certain students. My older sisters were beginning to fail and my grades were becoming lower. The municipality had to pay for children to move into the city school. The school board didn't want this money paid out, except for their own children. Maybe, they were thinking about keeping us uneducated and on the farms. Actually, many of the neighbour children did marry and stay on their parents' farms.

My parents fought this way of thinking by buying a house in Melville. The small house was originally owned by my grandfather, my dad's father. Mother had to get a job. She originally started cooking at a restaurant and later she took care of elderly patients in a senior's home.

Father continued to work on the farm. He drove out every day, both winter and summer, to look after the livestock and crops. That move put me in grade five at St. Henry's school.

Because mom was usually at work, my dad at the farm, and my sisters busy with their own activities, I had time to read and just be myself. On weekends, I would drive out to the farm with dad and have quiet time alone as well. I could once again spend endless hours in the world of my imagination. My only consternation at that time was the boy next door. He decided that he liked me and I was not used to attention. Much energy was spent ignoring him and pretending that he didn't exist. This ten-year-old girl was very uncomfortable. One evening, my sister and I were next door watching a show on their television set. He insisted on walking me home – only next door, and kissed me on the cheek. It felt very strange. Now, I felt that I had a mark that everybody could see. I was very upset and told him that he would never walk me home again. That was the absolute end, because I never talked to him or visited after that.

Going to a Catholic school until grade eight, kept my religious education up-to-date. We disliked being paraded over to the church for confession during the year. I always felt very uncomfortable and not quite sure what I should be saying. The girls had to put something on their head to cover their hair before leaving the school, if they happened to forget their hat. We were never given a reason as to why this was necessary. Church and religion were still not highly significant to me at that point due to lack of understanding.

Chores at home didn't allow me to get involved in after-school activities. My youngest sister was born just before we moved to Melville and she needed care. Whenever I was supposed to baby sit her, I would make excuses or not do a very good job of it, so I wasn't asked very often. I disliked entertaining little children. Teaching, in my mind, would be different than babysitting a younger sister. We were instructed to come home immediately from school and stay there until our parents came from work.

One Christmas, when I was in grade seven, our teacher, Sister Catherine, had a class vote to exchange presents. Everyone was excited. I knew that my family couldn't afford it but would have to try and accommodate what the class had decided. We drew each other's names from a hat. My parents were very helpful and understanding so, we purchased a present for one of my classmates. Finally the day of the class party arrived. Students began to give the presents to each person that they had selected earlier. I gave my present to one of the girls and she liked it. This made me feel happy inside. The end of the exchange came but, I had not received any present in return. Everyone seemed pleased with gifts such as hair pins, bath soaps, sports items, records, and a variety of things young people of that age treasure. When the class finally quieted down, and I had felt resigned that my name might have been misplaced, Sister Catherine spoke to us. She said, "Pat doesn't have her present yet and I had her name." She walked over to me with a package and I immediately burst into a smile with my good fortune. When I opened the gift, I saw an amazingly beautiful, framed picture of the Blessed Virgin Mary all surrounded in a light blue shade. Sister said that the picture was blessed which made it even more special. I was the luckiest student in the class that day. Now my daughter has that picture to keep. I want her to have something special that has a deep meaning to me.

When my older sister, Geri, at the age of thirteen, discovered boys, new problems began for my family. She started charging expensive clothes at the stores, borrowing or stealing money from my parent's wallets, and staying out late most of the night. Since we shared a bedroom, she would tell me some stories of drinking and reckless driving and ask me not to repeat them. Sometimes, she would climb up on the roof and knock on the window for me to let her in early in the morning. She was beginning to skip school constantly and her grades became lower. Eventually she started to fail.

I caught up to my sister in school at grade eight because I was still seriously learning and she wasn't. This year could be considered one of the toughest years of my life. Geri was popular with the class because she was beautiful and was involved in a crowd of high school students. It was unthinkable that her younger, nerdy sister should catch up with her. The girls made a point of excluding and ignoring me. I could face the world anyway, because I was proud that the popular girl was my sister. I wanted to be like her some day, no matter what happened. I was left out of pretty much everything, especially sports, not that I minded a whole lot. I wasn't the last one picked. I wasn't picked at all or allowed to play. I usually just stood and watched. If I was alone, nobody could be mean to me, hurt my feelings, or tease me. Yes, I was a victim of bullying in grade seven and eight, but mostly in grade eight until my sister ran away from home.

When my sister, Geri, left home, my parents didn't realize completely what was going on. They felt that she had left for Regina, but weren't sure. Mom and dad looked for help but, the police, school and the church would not help them. Life in the early 1960's wasn't as forgiving as it is in today's world. What my sister did by leaving home was unthinkable for any family member to do. My parents were devastated. The many conversations that I overheard while listening to them showed sorrow and frustration. Even though they remained strong for their girls at home, it was obvious that mom and dad were hurting horribly. Mom developed ulcers and hypertension. Dad never really said too much any more. The neighbour women and my aunts on the farm were really cruel to mom. They were never sympathetic and were very nosey. Every conversation they had with mom was to be judgmental and condemning. Our home had changed and would never return to the happy place that it once was.

I completed grade eight in Melville. The farm school closed that year and students were to be bussed to the city. My parents decided to sell the house in Melville and move our family back to the farm. It would be good to have our family in one house again. The highways were often treacherous and dad had been forced to drive out to the farm every day.

CHAPTER 2:

my car accident

I was now a grade nine, high school student. It didn't matter that I came to school by bus, because most of the students were bussed to Melville at that time. The trip was usually quite wild because our bus driver was in grade twelve at Melville High school. He was also popular and very good looking. He had a girlfriend that he was serious about but that didn't matter either. It was cool being on our bus because of the Public and Catholic student mix. We would discuss all the local gossip. The elementary kids sat at the back of the bus because they were fewer in number and overall quieter. The high school crowd had to discuss important news like, who was dating, when the next party would be held, and where it would be. I got dropped off at St. Henry's High school with the Catholic students.

My older sister, Sharryl, was popular with the bus crowd. She was invited to every party and included in whatever was happening. She had a serious boyfriend at that time. I was the younger sister left listening to the stories and wishing that I was older and could join in. My focus at this stage was learning to make myself more attractive. I would study what all the older girls were doing and how they were behaving. Makeup started being used every morning, as well as new hair styles. My selection of clothes increased because mom let me shop from the Sears catalogue when she could afford the purchases. The government provided a family allowance cheque of ten dollars a month that my parents let me keep. I was growing into a young teen girl and feeling better about my life.

Even though we now lived on the farm, many of the girls had been in my classes since grade five. I developed new friendships and became part of a group. Now that my sister, Geri, was gone, the girls welcomed me back among them. It was good to be discussing academics, movies, school dances, new students, etc. and not just sports continuously. Classes were offered with different groups of students at different times, which was also a big bonus. Sometimes, I would be invited to stay overnight at a friend's home and then have them stay at our house. We would always have fun staying up most of the night sharing gossip and news.

Being only fifteen-years-old, I was still really too young to be dating. That didn't stop me. In my mind, I was grown up. Everybody seemed to be paired up, or interested in somebody at that point, and I didn't want to miss out, or so I thought. One Friday, I was given permission to stay at my friend Maureen's house till dad came in for grocery shopping on Saturday. I would then get a ride home with him. It was a beautiful evening and Maureen and I decided to go for a walk after supper. She lived close to downtown Melville. The teenage nightlife included cruising Main Street. The music was always loud. There was usually yelling back and forth between the cars. You could meet anyone and everyone there. It just so happened, that one of the boys from our class was cruising with some friends. Doug shouted for us to meet up with him at the house behind the police station. We thought that it would be hilarious to be at a party behind the "cop shop".

When Maureen and I got there, it wasn't quite what we were expecting. There were a couple of girls who we didn't know but were older than us. There were mostly guys with beer and cigarettes in hand.

We were uncomfortable and wanted to leave because we really didn't know most of the people there. Doug decided that he was interested in spending time being near me. He offered me a beer and cigarette. I should have declined, but didn't. Maureen was trying a cigarette as well. I had smoked a cigarette with my sister, Geri before and felt that I knew about handling them. Dad had given us little tastes of beer and educated us on knowing when it was enough and not to have any more. I really thank him for that and did the same with my own children later in life. There are no alcoholics in our family. There was another young man at the party who was interested in me. I was too young and never should have been there in the first place. I told Martin that I had no interest in him and walked away. Anyway, after visiting with Doug it started getting late and we knew that Maureen's parents would be worried about us. We insisted that it was time to leave and were allowed to go with no pressure.

On Monday morning, I was back at school. Doug was in my home room class. He was giving me more attention than I wished for. Doug would glance over with smiles and whispers. He would send me secret messages and want to meet at break. I felt important because I was being noticed. Doug would want to meet on the weekend, if I could arrange to stay in Melville with friends. The problem with this friendship conflicted with my desire to get good grades. Time was being used on socializing and teen dating but, not on studying. Doug wasn't very serious about school at the time and wanted to convince me that he was going to be a famous drummer one day. Did he even own a set of drums or, know how to play them? There was never any evidence of it. I never fell for that story and eventually broke off the friendship. Ironically, I met up with him later when I was at university and spent a beautiful evening reminiscing. I didn't want to continue the friendship with him once again. You can just feel when it's not right and meant to be.

Fate was not meant to be denied. The young fellow named Martin decided to drive out to our farm the following Sunday after the party. He was alone in his car and came up the steps to knock on our door.

When I saw him, I couldn't believe that he would have the nerve to show up since I had only met him once before. He returned to his car to leave and my older sister, Sharryl came to see what was happening. When he saw her in the doorway, it must have been love at first sight. He connected with her and asked if he would be allowed to see her again. They mutually agreed. End of old boyfriend and beginning of new romance and marriage. They are still married and have been since 1967. I will get back to them later in the story.

My parents were not pleased that a guy should have come out to their farm for their second youngest daughter. Knowing that I was now beginning to date, they felt that Sharryl should take me along when she went to some of the parties and that way could watch over me. Another concern they had, was that one of our neighbours had a cousin named Michael who was about my age. He was impulsive and tended to take their farm truck. Michael would drive over to our place even though he was too young and did not have a driver's license. I was fearless and drove with him pretty much all over the road. He was not a good driver and my parents were afraid for my safety. When I started spending time with my older sister and future brother-in-law, I lost interest in Michael pretty quickly. I was now getting invited to parties at the different farms because I was hanging out with my sister. She would leave the farm with me, take me to whatever was happening, and drop me off. She would then ignore me and follow her own plans. I didn't mind because I soon came to realize that I could find my own attention. I started to be noticed by the other teens wherever we happened to be. If you talked, joked around, smoked and drank, the rest was easy. I began to find my own rides around the neighbourhood to parties. I preferred staying in a large group because it was more interesting and fun. Many times I would not get a ride home with the person that I left with but, pretty much didn't care.

I was really lost to my self at that time. I wasn't even thinking about God or, anything to do with my religion. I did the token go to Mass on Sunday, not really speaking for my whole family and their faith. Christmas and Easter were not celebrated as special religious events;

they were just slightly more than another day of the week. Mom and dad were still very unhappy with themselves and everything else going on in their lives. We were searching for my sister. Where was God at this time? Looking back, I know that he was still very much with us. Once again, there were so many times that he would protect us even though we didn't feel it at the time.

When Sharryl and Martin became engaged, I would still hang around with them. There always seemed to be some place to go and some people to meet up with. I made some new friends through Martin but was too young to think seriously about more than a casual afternoon of driving around, smoking cigarettes, and listening to loud music. My school grades were important to me and I needed to study. Tests were all based on memorization in those days.

The wedding of my sister, Sharryl to Martin took place in May of 1967 when I was sixteen-years-old. My aunt Frances, who was my mom's sister, thought I was much too young to be a bridesmaid and wouldn't know how to behave in a formal event. Of course, I had to prove her wrong. The wedding was beautiful and I was a model of decorum. In fact, many family members commented on my appearance and behaviour. I wanted my sister to be proud of me and not regret her choice.

Several months after the wedding, we got word about my missing sister, Geri. She was living with a Metis man, named Paul, in Regina. She also had a son, Gerald and was pregnant again. She was only seventeen years old. Paul was not employed and providing a living from questionable means. Their apartment was in a condemned building and consisted of two rooms. I hadn't seen Geri in several years and was terribly excited to do so. She was my sister and I really admired the way she was able to do things. She knew how to style her own hair better than the hairdressers and use make-up to enhance her beauty at all times. Geri was caring for a baby, looking after her own home by making curtains, cushions, and decorating with whatever she could afford and I loved everything about her. I always wished that I could be like her. She was my mentor and my idea of perfection.

That year, at Christmas, Geri, Paul and family finally came home to the farm. We were waiting for their arrival on Christmas Eve. They were driving from Regina on a cold, dark evening with the vehicle that they owned. Their car was loaded with Christmas presents, their suitcases and belongings, a baby and all his care items, plus she was seven-months pregnant. The phone rang long distance from Grenfell. While they were driving down the highway, their car started on fire. They were able to escape with their lives and possessions, but the vehicle was completely destroyed. The people that were traveling behind them noticed the flames under the automobile and managed to warn them to stop their car in time. Some kind and thoughtful strangers drove them and all their possessions to the nearest town before continuing on their own way. Dad and I drove from our farm to Grenfell that night to get them. I was as excited as I could possibly be. We had a great Christmas, despite the earlier mishaps. Mom and dad helped them get back to Regina by bus. Mom also sent all sorts of food, clothes, and anything she felt that they could possibly use.

I was allowed to go to Regina to visit with my sister Geri. Her home by today's standards was inadequate, but it seemed large to me. She even had electricity and running water. I had my first bath in a huge bathtub since I was a child. The feeling of luxury and joy can't possibly be described. I spent a long time just soaking and feeling like a queen. My sister, Geri and I, could spend hours of time talking and being together. We never seemed to run out of conversation. We drank cups of coffee and smoked cigarettes together. She treated me as an adult and best friend. I really loved her as a confidant.

A couple of months later, in February, my sister gave birth to another son, Paul Jr. He was premature and very tiny. Geri had the baby when expected, but she was so thin and unhealthy that the baby was only a few pounds. My sister barely weighed a hundred pounds. In fact, during her Christmas visit Geri was wearing a narrow skirt and you would never have guessed that she was even pregnant. Paul Jr. had to stay in the hospital for some time after the delivery. My sister was a good mother and took care of her two boys with all the love she had.

She did her very best with what she knew and with whatever means she had available to her. I was asked to be Paul Jr.'s godmother when he was baptized. I wasn't able to go to Regina for the event but my name was written down as his godmother. That was special to me.

During a visit to her house in Regina that summer, Geri encouraged me to go swimming to the city outdoor pool. My future brother-in-law's two nieces were visiting and had been good swimmers from childhood. They were willing to teach me how to swim. I had never been to the pool since we visited the lake once a year as a family as I was growing up. Wearing my swimsuit and with a towel in hand we excitedly ventured to the public swimming pool. I was very determined to learn to swim that day. The girls showed me some swimming strokes and I practiced them. After many practice trials, I became quite confident in myself. I decided to move my swim lesson to the deep end of the pool without telling anyone. I dived into the water. My newly practiced swim strokes were not working. I found myself near the bottom of the swimming pool and near drowning. I was beginning to panic and felt intense fear. Suddenly, I was grabbed by the arms and pulled to the surface. With much coughing and choking, I started to feel like I could breathe again. Sadly, after that day, I never felt like learning to swim. Everything that I attempted came with a struggle. I thank you God that I didn't drown that day.

Meanwhile, time is passing in my teen years. Both of my older sisters are now married and living in Regina. I am seventeen-years-old and in grade eleven. I am the oldest daughter at home, going to high school, and wishing I was living in Regina as well. I was occasionally dating a friend of my brother-in-law's from Yorkton. I know that he was more serious about our friendship than I was. I liked the idea that I was dating more than the reality of it.

During the time of my mid teens, God returned into my life with more meaning than I could have ever anticipated. I was mainly focused on school, dating, and visiting with my sisters. God was playing a minor role in my thoughts. The specific incident that would change everything happened on the Mother's day Sunday in May. Richard, the guy I was dating, made arrangements for us to drive to Regina and stay with Sharryl and Martin for the weekend. The time was awesome because we drove to Buffalo Pound Lake and had a picnic, went to a movie at night and just had a fun visit. The Sunday went by quickly and it was time to leave for the farm. We were driving in Richard's brand new Envoy Epic car. It was a small vehicle, but he was an experienced truck driver. After about an hour on the road, Richard suggested that I should take the wheel for a while. I had my Learner's License and had driven my dad's car on the farm. I really didn't feel comfortable but he kept insisting that it would be good experience for me to get some highway driving. He would be right beside me.

The two-lane highway was not divided. It was known to be busy with weekend traffic consisting of both trucks (some very large) and cars. The wind was very strong that afternoon. The late day sun was shining towards my eyes. We were proceeding to Melville at the sixty-mile-per-hour speed limit. A large semi-trailer truck was approaching me from the opposite direction. When the semi truck passed by, the vacuum from behind the vehicle pulled me partly into the other lane. There was a station wagon coming at us mostly head-on. Richard grabbed the steering wheel to try and bring his car back into the proper lane. Unfortunately, he steered too far and the two passenger side wheels caught on the loose gravel. The car traveled at a slant down into the ditch. Meanwhile, I was gradually applying the brakes. We would have gone down into the ditch without any damage, but came upon an approach for a side road. There was a drainage culvert dug into the road. When the vehicle that I was driving struck the approach, the front driver's wheel impacted into the culvert. We struck solid and moved no further. Later, I learned that I had reduced the speed to twenty-miles-per-hour, but we did not wear seat belts in that time period. With a seat belt, I would have only experienced minor injuries.

Richard was not hurt at all. I smashed my face into the steering wheel and the window crank had lodged partly into my left calf muscle. Everything had happened in a split second. Richard opened his door, got out, and came over to where I was collapsed over the steering wheel. I wasn't feeling anything and unaware that I was even hurt. He opened the driver's door and pulled me out. Richard stood me up on the side of the road and repeated over and over, "Are you all right?" At that moment, blood came gushing from my nose all over my clothes and the road. The people that were in the station wagon, coming head on towards our vehicle had pulled over to the side of the road. They ran to us and laid me down on the ground with my head slightly elevated so that I wouldn't choke on the blood. They found a huge towel in their car and put it over my face.

Meanwhile, I was not aware of all these proceedings. I learned about them later on. I was in my own world. I suppose that you could call it shock. I could only think about God at that time. In my mind I pictured that I was with Him and wanted to stay in the beautiful place that I was experiencing. I believed that I could be there forever with God. I wanted to die in the worst way. I did not want to come back to reality. The place wasn't visual. Everything was just a blank white. I could only hear muffled sounds in the distance. The pull of belonging came from the feeling that I was experiencing from within. I had never felt that peaceful and wrapped in love my whole life. I prayed and wished with the strongest desire ever to stay there. It was not meant to be because reality returned and along with it came the pain. Amazingly, after that I kept thinking about God being strongly present in my life again.

The people that I had almost injured put me in their station wagon. I was transported to the Balcarres hospital. There I had six stitches put into the top of my smashed nose. I was starting to see bruises pop up all over me. When I walked out of the emergency room into the waiting area, I could see my swollen face in the mirror. Did you ever cry with your whole nose packed, bandaged and taped? Don't do it. It only makes everything feel worse. I had to stop crying and just asked the nurse if I would stay that way. She thoughtfully assured me that everything would heal. Dad came at that time and drove me back to Melville for observation in the hospital, which would last a week.

While I was recovering in the hospital, two more tragedies occurred. The first one happened with my four and a half year old cousin, Darlene. She was involved in a farm accident, on the Monday and she died almost immediately. She ran to meet her father who was coming into the farm yard from working in the field. He did not see her. She got caught under a grain auger and it rolled over her body. Mom always remembered and related what she strangely noticed on the afternoon of my Sunday car accident. She had set a lunch table for a group of little girls all laughing and enjoying themselves with Darlene among them. Mom never had a lunch experience like this before.

The second accident involved a young biker cousin and friend of my brother-in-law Martin, a day later. Clarke was driving to Melville from Canora to visit his girlfriend. Linda had his child, a boy, who was less than a year old. She was pregnant with their second child. We lived a few miles apart at the farm and knew each other very well. Clarke and Linda were planning to be married in the near future. He was driving to her farm late that night and may have fallen asleep behind the steering wheel of his car. The vehicle that Clarke was driving smashed into the concrete guard rail of a bridge. The car was totally destroyed and he was dead at the scene.

The day after I was released from hospital, I attended both funerals. Darlene was buried in the morning and Clarke in the afternoon. During Darlene's morning funeral, my aunt asked my mother "why did my child get killed in an accident and not yours?" The question made my mother very upset. The second funeral for Clarke was just as upsetting. It took place in the Ukranian Catholic Church in Yorkton. The funeral seemed endless and the temperature was extremely hot in the building. We returned to our friend Linda's parents' farm in the evening after the funeral. We all needed to comfort each other. Linda told us about the night that Clarke was killed. She was awakened after hearing him call her name in the farm yard the exact time that his accident happened. She went outdoors but of course there was nobody there.

My body continued to heal itself after my own accident. The swelling and bruising on my skin soon disappeared. There was minor surgery on my leg, but that wasn't too bad. The doctor told me that I would have problems with mobility as I aged. I really didn't care or think about problems that could result during my old age at that time. I soon returned to finish grade eleven in school and found the teachers very kind and compassionate. Finally, the June exams were completed and I managed to continue maintaining good grades.

Two more incidents happened with Richard shortly after. The first was an accident where Richard was driving his mother's car. We were pulling out of a strip mall in Yorkton onto the main street. He didn't check for oncoming traffic, but proceeded to drive. A vehicle collided into the driver's side of the car. I wasn't injured, but was just shaken up. I was taken to the hospital and checked out but only had minor bumps and bruises. It was the continued fear and shaking through my whole body afterwards that was the problem. I felt that they would never stop. Now, Richard's car and his mother's car are both in the vehicle repair shop. One night a week later, Richard came to Melville with a friend to drive me back to Yorkton. When we got to Yorkton, we just drove around listening to music. Suddenly, Richard's friend recognized someone who pulled up beside the car and challenged him to a drag race. He accelerated and began speeding much too fast. I was terrified. The friend suddenly remembered that he wanted to turn on the highway to Melville. There is a lazy curve and the highway was still under construction. He sped up to cut the other driver off. Then, he started skidding into the ditch. The car was tugging at the loose gravel as it swayed. It felt like a mighty hand was holding our car onto the road. We stopped the vehicle. The wheel skid marks were unbelievable. There was a finger's width of distance from the ditch embankment. It was a miracle that we didn't roll over and get badly injured or even killed. I was again shaking from head to foot. I remained super quiet until we reached my parent's farm. When I got out of the car, I told Richard that I never, ever, wanted to see him again. He never did return to see me after this incident. That was the end of this scary time of my life. I knew that God had spared me from all the disaster that I had been through. All I really wanted to do was to be back with my family and friends again.

Grade twelve was one of my favourite school years. I started dating a very nice guy named Gordon. He was kind, thoughtful, and treated me with respect. I knew that I would never be really serious with him because I wanted to go to university and become a teacher. He wanted to be a farmer and had minimum education. Weekdays were spent at school and studying in the evenings, with some farm chores to do. On the weekends, there was time for visiting and partying. We had loads of fun with sleigh riding parties, wiener roasts, going to the drive in movie theatre, playing miniature golf, driving around in the country, etc. I felt the effects of my accident but everyone was kind to me. I attended Sunday Mass and the sacraments. Praying every night became something that I wouldn't miss. I started talking to God seriously with a grateful heart and loving Him for allowing me to survive. I knew how fortunate I was to be able to move forward with my life while others didn't have the chance any more.

It was during my grade twelve year that I began to feel that God could be talking to me. It wasn't a sudden discovery but just a knowing that could not have possibly come from anywhere else. There is no other way that I could have known events that were going to occur in the future. I knew that one day I was going to have a child and that this first baby was to be a boy. The child would die before or soon after it was born. Not knowing about angel and human creation differences, I believed that he would become an angel of God. It didn't really bother me at the time because I thought it was my own imagination that was creating this from some inner fear. I could ignore it and it would just disappear. I believed that I had read this in a Bible story about the eldest sons being killed during the time of Moses and even Jesus as a baby. The strange part was that this "knowing" never entirely disappeared and continued to erupt in my mind spontaneously. The "knowing" would repeat and repeat for many years to come. I was lead to believe that all future children would be healthy and I would never have to go through the death of a child again. Is it that you really know something or, are you dwelling on an inner fear that would probably never happen? I preferred to think of this as my own imagination.

What grade twelve teen girl is going to worry about a baby dying when she has years of school ahead and is not even experiencing a serious relationship? My mind totally ignored that thought and feeling. Besides, I was finally finished high school and was accepted at the University of Regina in an education program. I had everything that I could possibly dream of. I was moving to Regina and leaving the farm in Melville for good. I broke off the friendship with Gordon feeling that I was now starting a new time in my life. Mom and dad had arranged for me to move in with my sister Sharryl when the school year started in the fall. In order to pass the time, I convinced dad to let me paint the exterior of our farm house. I put two coats of yellow paint on the siding. I was not allowed to do the roof though because dad felt that it would be too dangerous. It did help make the time pass quickly and soon it was time to pack and leave.

CHAPTER 3:

university years

Facing university enrollment was a monumental task. There were classes in many different buildings that consisted of several floors each. Plus, the buildings were scattered all over the campus. There were no indoor hallways between the buildings in those days, except for the Classroom building, the Library and Laboratory building. It was even difficult to tell when one building ended and another began. Registration meant going to all the various locations where the class departments existed. In other words, to register for Education classes, you went to the Education building, Arts classes required registration in the Classroom building, and Science classes meant registering in the Laboratory building, etc. Merely finding my way around the university was a challenge at first. There were many different religious community sects to be cautious of. Some groups wore robes of white and had unusual haircuts. Many booths were set up in the hallways with members encouraging students to enroll with them. The air at the university was usually thick with cigarette smoke, mixed with other odours. The whole experience was somewhat new and frightening.

When I moved into my sister Sharryl's home, I realized that she was very cramped for space. She had a two bedroom house with one bathroom. One bedroom was their master and was used for their newborn daughter as well. The second bedroom, I shared with her weekly laundry. Most of the bedroom space and half of the bed was covered in the clothing and linens/towels that needed to be returned to their cupboards and closets. I had no space for books and no place to hang my clothes, so they had to stay in my suitcase or on a neat pile placed on the floor. There was no space available for privacy or doing any school work. The arrangement was not going to work for a long term. I loved being with my sister and little niece, Lori, though because she was now my godchild as well. I was honoured to be godmother to both a nephew and a niece.

Classes began soon upon arrival. Everything was new and needed extra time for the adjustment process. I was overwhelmed by the workload and didn't feel prepared to meet the challenge. Yet, I was determined to persist by attending all classes and striving to do my best. When I left the campus, fear would set in and I did not wish to return the next day. I would force myself to be at every class. Everyone at the university seemed so much brighter and more intelligent than me. I wanted to make friends because I believed that other students should be in the same position as I was, but that wasn't happening. Other students appeared to have friends already, and I felt left out. Between classes, I would sit alone in a certain spot far away from anyone else. I was quite good at feeling sorry for myself. I was afraid and very uncomfortable. In the evenings, I didn't study much because there were too many distractions at my sister's small home.

Part way through the first semester, my sister Geri ended up in the hospital with Gall stones. She had surgery at the General hospital which was on the way home from the university. I stopped in to visit with her one day after classes. While I was there talking with her, I explained how staying with Sharryl wasn't working for me. Geri encouraged me to gather all my belongings and move in with her, Paul and the children. Their family had moved to another location since I had started university. They were living in a large house and I could have my own bedroom for privacy and studying. My parents were providing Sharryl with food from the farm and some money for accommodating me. She was meant to forward me the money for bus fare and other personal needs. Occasionally, I would get a small amount of cash but it didn't meet all my expenses. My parents had paid the tuition for the first semester but didn't realize how expensive university was going to be. They didn't factor in that even the textbooks were extremely expensive. I knew that Geri and Paul were struggling financially with their two small children and now having me in their house would make matters worse. They never complained or made me feel unwelcome. We managed with what was available.

One morning on my way to class, I noticed that I was short one cent of the ten cent bus fare. I put the nine coins in the slot and frantically thought the bus driver would know. He could ask me to leave the bus and walk. It didn't happen even though I felt guilty the entire ride. Another morning, I didn't have bus fare at all and chose to hitch-hike a ride on Broad Street. Other students would get rides this way all the time. One car stopped and all the students waiting there piled into it. There was no room for me. Another car stopped but I was standing alone. The man encouraged me to get in for a free ride to the university. As we were driving along Wascana Parkway, he began putting his hand on my knee. I removed it. He put it back. I asked to be let out. He said, "Every time you get in a car with a stranger, you are taking a chance. I won't bother you because you are afraid but be smart and don't take chances like that." I knew that my life had to change. This arrangement was not going to work for very long. I did love living with my favourite sister though. Yet, I felt the need to be more independent and have a more stable income.

Within a couple of months, I learned that Gordon had moved to Regina. He wanted to continue dating but I had lost total interest in him and didn't want to see him. I really intended to cut all ties with my past. Gordon found a job working for a roofing company. When he believed that he could change my mind and encourage me to return with him to the farm, I had to state my case firmly and with finality. Almost a year later, he became discouraged and returned to his parent's farm without me. I had a long journey ahead. Gordon didn't fit into my new plans for the future. We really were not right for each other and I knew it. I had made a couple of new friends with some girls in my classes during the second semester and began to feel better. Geri lent me some of her stylish clothes and I was feeling attractive once again.

Towards early spring, Geri and Paul had to move again because the house they were renting was being sold. My second semester was almost completed when we all moved to an apartment house on Rae Street. Geri, Paul, and the boys would live on the main floor. I would have a small light-housekeeping room on the second floor. During this move my maternal grandmother passed away in Melville. I was given a few of her old dishes, pots, cutlery, linens and towels to stock my cupboards. My sister gave me an old lift-the-flap toaster and I was ready to begin living on my own. Everything that I owned fit into a round, yellow washbowl that I still possess as a reminder of the possessions I started with. At this point, mom and dad were still sending some money for rent. I had taken a student loan for tuition fees and books in the second semester. One evening though, when I decided to stop by Sharryl's house for a visit, I didn't realize how hungry I appeared. When she saw me, my sister gave me a few coins to buy myself something to eat. She said that I looked starved, pale and ready to faint. Food was a luxury that I quite often had to do without. I couldn't disagree with her for it had been a couple of days since I had eaten. Hunger was something that became a constant part of my life but a person gets used to little or no food. The lack of food was very contradictory to having lived on the farm with large amounts of fresh food available.

As soon as I moved into my small room, I learned that some members of the Apollo Motorcycle gang were living in the basement. At first I was afraid to come and go from my residence. It helped that my sister was living in the same building. She assured me that if I avoided them, made no eye contact, and didn't say anything, they would not pay any attention to me. They would roar up in front of our three-storey converted house. The men would be wearing their helmets, boots, shirts, and gang-decorated leather vests. They looked very intimidating and tough. It felt like I was a brave soul, just to be living there. The days went by and her advice proved true. There was an invisible agreement of respect and space. Soon I was no longer afraid and realized that I was free to come and go without being bothered at all.

The second semester came to an end and I managed to keep my average high enough to continue in education. It had been rough doing school work while being hungry most of the time. Usually, I managed to have two small meals per day. Many times I would get behind on assignments and reports but arranged to get extensions after talking to the professor. One professor compassionately passed me with a higher grade than I deserved after talking with me in his office. He questioned me about my personal life and I didn't want to lie to him. He just shook his head in disbelief. I couldn't understand what his problem was. My life seemed normal and regular to me. He saw all the things that I failed to realize and wished to help me. I didn't think that I needed anybody's help. Thanks to his caring, I was able to continue in my education program.

Now I had a tough decision to make. I had to either get a summer job or else move back to my parent's farm. My greatest fear was about finances for immediate living expenses and for the future. I knew that if I went back to the farm, my parent's could not afford to have me return to university in the fall. I could take another student loan but that would mostly cover the cost of tuition and books. I would still need to find money for food and a room. I really wanted to work and not return to the farm at all. There was no way that I could be happy living a farm life even though lots of my girl friends from high school were married and doing just that.

I had a time frame of about two weeks to find work, if I could. That was when my rent would terminate and I had already given notice. As luck would have it, I got a phone call for a job working in Regina Beach at a restaurant. I thought that I would be cooking in the kitchen making hamburgers, corn on the cob, hotdogs, eggs, etc. and living at the beach for the summer. When my new boss drove up to the building that I was living in, he saw the bike gang out front by the steps. He couldn't believe his eyes and questioned me about everything. He was not convinced that the living arrangement was safe and honourable. I could feel that he proceeded to judge me unfavourably. He probably employed me at the time because he needed somebody and decided to give me a chance without having to look any further.

Living at Regina Beach was a blast at first. There is something about the atmosphere of living in a resort area that is thrilling for a young person. Besides meeting the two university girls that were working at the restaurant, other girls were employed at the various businesses. There were large numbers of men around the village in the evenings working for a road construction crew and a pipeline crew. The few girls working in the restaurant were never without male attention, in fact too much of it most of the time. I spent most of my time working in the back kitchen so I missed out on a lot of the excitement. I could be seen washing huge piles of dishes from the daily customers. The restaurant didn't have a dishwasher and I couldn't keep up with the cooking and dishes during the daily working hours. As a result, when my shift was over the expectation was for me to stay until everything was cleaned up, without any compensation.

There was one guy, Pete, who would wait in the diner until I was finished work. He seemed quite nice and had noticed me working alone in the back kitchen. I never seemed to catch up with the work and generally worked late. Pete seemed sincere about getting to know me better and I welcomed his attention. He was working on the pipeline crew. Strangely, he told me that he played drums with a band. As I got to know him a little better, he started to pressure me into an intimate relationship. He wanted me to trust him and that he cared about me. I tend to not trust very easily. I felt that I barely knew him at all and that he was deceiving me about the drums. Red flags began to rise from the feeling of being lied to about another drummer from the past. The spirit within me may have been protecting me from an unsafe relationship because Pete eventually lost interest in me. When I met another fellow afterwards, from the road construction crew, the feeling of mistrust happened again. I would have made a mistake to allow that friendship also.

One evening Pete and I were out walking around the resort. Some young adults about our age were having an outdoor, backyard party. When we arrived, they were talking and telling jokes. They ushered us to a lawn chair that was placed in a large circle with all the others. We were offered a drink of alcohol. Marijuana was being passed around in the circle. Everybody would take a drag and pass the joint on to the next person. I had never used any drugs, except for alcohol and tobacco. I didn't want to try the marijuana and would discreetly pass it on. Someone noticed and tried to coax me to try it, calling me a chicken. Some inner voice told me to stay away from what I was uncomfortable with. The Holy Spirit protected me from the taking of drugs with a deep sense of discomfort from inside. I was the only person at that party that did not do the drugs. There was never any remorse, but a deep gratitude that I was protected from some bad mistakes. This was a time of learning, and I would not have survived tremendous hurt without the guidance of the Holy Spirit. I just followed my conscience. Looking back I know for sure that God was with me.

A month and a half after moving to Regina Beach, one of the ladies waiting on tables was told that she was no longer needed. She should pack her belongings and she would be given a ride to Regina on Saturday morning. She seemed to be handling the bad news quite well. My employer did not tell me that I was being terminated as well. On that Saturday morning, he walked up to me and asked me where my suitcase was. At that moment I found out that I was being driven back to Regina. He did not give any reason for my dismissal. I never found out what I had done wrong. All I could think about and feel was the fear of once more being unemployed. The bosses' niece took my position the following day. Apparently, my help was only needed until the high school year was finished

My now ex-boss drove me into Regina and dropped me off, with my suitcase, at the corner of Broad Street and Victoria Avenue. I had no place to go. I refused to go back to live with my sisters. There had been enough difficulties placed on them previously because they tried to help me. It wasn't going to work. I was given eighty dollars for about two months of employment, the time that I had worked in the restaurant. The remainder of my earned money, the employer felt comfortable keeping for room and board. What was I going to do? I could catch the bus and go back to the farm. That would only be a backup plan in desperation. If I returned to the farm, I remembered that the chances were extremely small of having the funding and opportunity to return. I needed time to think.

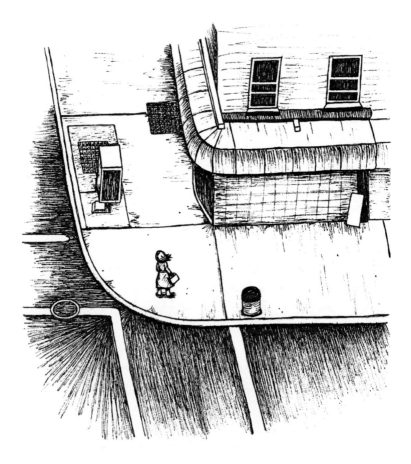

Being hungry and close to a downtown restaurant, I decided to go inside. It was dim in the interior and I searched for an empty booth. I sat down in the booth by myself. The waiter came and offered me a menu. I glanced over the entries but knew that I could only afford a small plate of fries and a soda. A girl, who I barely recognized but looked somewhat familiar, walked in from the street. She sat down across from me and asked, "Do you mind if I join you?" I didn't know her name and tried to remember where I had seen her before. The waiter came. I placed my order without really looking at her too closely. She introduced herself as Linda and said that she had a summer job at Sask.-Tel. She had been in my Philosophy class. I told Linda my sad story. She couldn't believe that someone could be as cruel as my boss had been. Linda suggested that I could crash at her place for a couple of days and try for another job. I would be asked to leave if her landlord found out that I was staying with her. She had a light-housekeeping suite on Lorne Street. I didn't have any choice and appreciated the offer. I accepted even though I felt guilty about the deception to her landlord.

I stayed with Linda and began the job search on Monday morning. There was a government employment center for teens called "Teen Power" that I put my request with. Two days later they offered me a guaranteed one day job at the University of Regina, Physical Plant. I was to help with inventory. My job was to count electrical and plumbing supplies on a tally sheet. Two university students were hired for the possible two day job, depending on the speed with which we worked. There was another girl who showed up for work with me that morning. Our workplace was the fourth floor of the Classroom building and we were put to work doing the inventory assignment. It was somewhat boring, but I was certainly not complaining. I was ecstatic just to be earning a day's pay and probably a second day's pay as well. The other girl did not look pleased because she felt the work was below her ability.

The second day, I showed up for work but the other girl did not. She informed them that she had another job. I began to work immediately because the men working in that department wanted the inventory done quickly. Being the only girl with all those male employees was pretty cool. They soon started treating me like a little sister and spoiling me with kindness. They would offer me coffee, snacks and their cigarettes. Everyone smoked at work in those days. The work was completed all too soon and I had nothing left to do after the lunch break. The foreman suggested that I could do a tally of the results from the worksheets.

That afternoon, I was moved to work on the fourth floor of the Education building in the Physical Plant office. Everything was wonderful, plus I was hired to come back for a few more days work. Rosemary, the office secretary, trained me to answer the phone. I knew how to type. She showed me how to assign work to the various male trade people over the walkie-talkie system throughout the university. I was unbelievably happy and inadvertently being trained to take over the office when Rosemary took her three week vacation. My favourite part was assigning the jobs to the Physical Plant male employees and they liked hearing my voice over their radios. They started joking with me and soon became my group of friends all over the university. The tradesmen would show me interesting things like how to make keys and pick locks, where the hidden crawl spaces were under the buildings, how the big boilers operated to heat and cool the buildings, etc. The office work did require me to now dress the part and look my best. No more blue jeans for the summer. I couldn't believe how my life had changed from being dumped on the street downtown with nothing but my suitcase to now working in a university office for the entire remaining summer holiday. Do you think that God was looking after me? I do. I made sure to pray every night, spend time talking to God about my problems no matter where I was, and thanking Him all the time. Sometimes, it was only in my mind depending where I was or who I was with. The problems of any day would sort themselves out whenever I asked God to help me.

Meanwhile, I am still sneaking living accommodations with Linda. The University of Regina only pays its employees once a month, after it has been worked. I could get a partial advance and that went to pay for rent. Yes, the landlord discovered me a couple of days after I moved in. He agreed to let Linda and I share the upper room when it became available at the end of the month. The rent was at a higher rate now because there were two people. Linda had some money for the rent with little left over. I hadn't been paid enough for food after I paid my portion of the rent. We were both struggling that month. I remember having a jar of rhubarb preserves from my sister. Linda could buy some bread and a couple of other food items. For most of two weeks, that's all the food we had to live on. She had some friends at work who shared their lunch with her, but I always felt hungry. I wanted to ration our small supply of food equally. We joked that when we both finally got a full paycheck, we would go to "L'habitant", which was a very expensive restaurant close to our home. We did make it there after I got my first paycheck. Linda and I looked at the menu prices and had to share the cheapest food order that they offered. It was fun anyway and we were getting along great.

After the three week employment in the Physical Plant office, Maintenance Department, I was moved over to the Physical Plant director's office. There I got to answer phones, do some filing, and serve coffee during meetings. I still couldn't believe how my life had moved into such a wonderful direction. God had taken me from cooking and feeling totally unappreciated to now working in a director's office with great people who made me feel competent and wonderful. I can honestly say that the move was a scary one though because I felt very under qualified.

During the employment in the Physical Plant Maintenance office, I learned about a second job that I could do in the evenings during the week. I was hired to clean an office building on Albert Street. When I would get off work at the university office, I would catch the bus to my sister's house. There, Jim, my sister's neighbour, would give me a ride to the building on Albert Street and we would work from five to nine in the evening. The next morning, I would start work again at 8:30a.m. At the University office I needed to be dressed appropriately once again. Then, I would work until 4:30p.m.and rush once more to catch the bus, change clothes, and get to my evening job. I was becoming exhausted and very worn out. From having no employment, I now had too much. One morning, the Director of Maintenance, noticed that I was looking extremely overtired. He asked about my situation and I told him that I hoped to work at an evening job for the next semester. That way, I would have some money to pay for food and rent. I would still need a student loan for tuition fees. He advised me to quit the evening job and he would employ me with the cleaning staff at the university. I would be able to take classes and work at the same place. Wow!! I was feeling extremely fortunate. Needless to say, I accepted.

The living arrangement was working well for Linda and me. I was at the university most of the time and hardly ever there. Linda was a great friend but she loved to leave a mess behind. Most of her clothes resided on the back of a kitchen chair. She left her dirty dishes on the table. Linda would often spit sunflower seeds in our one sink and add her cigarette butts there too. The sink was plugged most of the time. I only managed to clean up after myself, which was easy since I had so little to clean. Linda's disaster increased every day but I really didn't care at all. We both loved the same loud music, especially The Animals, the Beatles, the Rolling Stones, Credence Clearwater Revival, etc. We both smoked cigarettes, and she lent me her awesome buckskin jacket with the long tassels which went well with jeans. I had long hair and had strands of beads around my neck. This farm girl was no longer a nerd. During the day, I was an office secretary very well dressed with the two dresses I owned and after work I got to pretend I was a cool hippie.

The friendship between Linda and I grew every day. It was hard to believe that she knew so many people and I got to meet them now that my evenings were free from work. A memorable time was on an evening when we took the bus to the horse race track at the exhibition grounds. Linda knew a family that was in the harness racing circuit. We had a grand time visiting in the barn while the evening wore on. It eventually got to the time for us to leave. That was when one of the horse drivers, Paul, asked me to pack up and join the circuit. I could travel with him, have some adventures, and stay for free. He promised me plenty of excitement and lots of new people to meet. That inner voice, didn't agree with the offer. It said, "What happens when the summer is over and racing is finished? You would have to give up your job and everything that you just worked so hard for. You wouldn't have any place in Regina when you returned. What will you do for money? Do you really think this guy is going to support you? What happens if you don't get along or get tired of each other? Can you live with yourself when you wake up tomorrow? Do you really trust this stranger that you just met?" My conscience won out and I said a definite "NO". I never saw him again because they moved on to the next city. It was still fun tracking him in the newspaper though and having known him for the evening. I never thought until later, what sort of impact my disappearance would have had on my family. When would they have realized that I was missing?

One day, I returned home from the University office very relieved that it was Friday. Linda wasn't home from her job yet. There was a stranger in our apartment. The lady looked at least five years older than us and very authoritative. When I opened the door, she asked me who I was. I told her. She said that she was Linda's older sister. She stated, "I believed that Linda lived alone. I am going to be staying here with her for the weekend. I don't know how she can live with you when you are such a messy pig." My jaw dropped with disbelief. She was accusing me of her sister's mess. When I tried to defend myself, she started yelling at me. At that point, Linda came into the room. She hugged her sister and welcomed her. Apparently, when Linda introduced us I learned that her sister was a psychiatric nurse. At that point, I lost respect for the profession. Since Linda and I only had a sofa that became a bed when the back was folded down, there would not be room for three people in the one room suite. I was the odd man out and really did not want to stay anyway. Linda never owned her mess. She allowed her sister to continue believing that the mess was mine.

Linda had lived in the apartment building for some time and knew all the other girls living there. She went down to the second level and asked Carolyn if I could spend the next couple of days with her. I went down and got introduced to Carolyn. We liked each other instantly. Within the two days, Linda told me that she was moving to live with her sister. I now needed a roommate. I couldn't afford the upstairs room and Carolyn's apartment was too small for two people. We decided to move upstairs. Carolyn would be my new roommate. She asked one thing of me. Carolyn had been engaged to Jim but for some reason, they decided to end the relationship. She said that she still had feelings for him. Carolyn made me promise that when I met him, and if I dated him, that I would never get serious about him. Carolyn said that it would bother her too much. I promised.

Carolyn worked as a car-hop at the A & W on North Albert Street. She was meeting many of the young police recruits that were frequenting her place of work. Her main ambition was to be invited to a graduation. The real neat thing was police recruits at that time had to be single men. Married men were not allowed into the Royal Canadian Mounted Police program. We knew for sure that the guys were single and not married men. Carolyn started inviting some of her new police friends up to our apartment and I would come home from work to find them there. I told her quite clearly that I did not want to date any guy with a shaved head of hair when I was trying to be a hippie. I also never wanted to be serious or marry any man that would one day be out on a highway where he could be killed or shot at. I was very adamant about this. That was when I met Gregg. I told you about him in the first chapter. How could this young recruit be so wonderful and attractive at the same time? He was polite to a fault, came from a military family, took me to nice restaurants, and treated me better than I could have ever dreamed. It was a fairy tale time with him, and then his graduation. I borrowed a formal gown from Carolyn and had my hair done at a salon for that day. She was totally, happy for me and slightly jealous in a good way. Of course, such happiness can't last. I had forgotten my intention to never be serious about a police recruit.

My second year of university in the Education program was now beginning. During the time that I was working in the Physical plant director's office, I was offered room and board for a minimal charge.

The main office manager, Jill, asked if I would move into her home for a year while her husband traveled to an out of town teaching job. He would be gone during the week and return home on the weekends. She would not have to spend all this time alone, she would be helping me, and we could both travel to the university together by bus in the morning. The offer was very good, so I took it. It also meant that I would be moving out of the suite that I was sharing with Carolyn. She knew so many people, that Carolyn was able to find another roommate immediately. Carolyn and I promised to keep in touch because we both really liked each other and got along so well. I knew that I would miss her but needed to have the stability of room and board. It would be easier to concentrate on my studies at Jill's house. This semester was leading into actual teaching practicum. I was no longer just sitting in classrooms to observe.

Life, for me, seems to always lead in the wrong direction. Carolyn's past fiancé, Jim, was working at the university and taking classes. We seemed to be crossing paths continuously and eventually he asked me out. We enjoyed each other's company and had long walks and wonderful conversations. Jim started offering me a ride to the university and we would have lunch together. He was a very wonderful person and someone that I could really care for, if it went unchecked. We knew many of the same people and spent endless hours at the university. There was one huge problem. I had made a promise and I intended to keep it. It would not be fair to Carolyn if it would bother her so much.

One beautiful, sunny afternoon, Jim and I were walking through Victoria Park in downtown Regina. We were talking and laughing about many things. The conversation had taken many twists and turns but we were having a great time. We stopped to sit down on one of the benches for a few moments. Jim looked over at me with an extremely serious look. He wanted our friendship to reach another level. Jim had become serious about me and I knew that I could have stronger feelings for him. I had made a promise that was continuously haunting my mind. I couldn't go back on my word. Why did I have to be in this predicament? There was no choice. I had to let the moment and my feelings go. I told him that I only could be friends with him and that it would never get any more serious than that. We stayed as friends for a while longer. I made a point of making excuses and starting to date again. After all, Carolyn never needed to know about Jim and me. Strangely, years later, I learned that he was not the man God intended for me. My option was that Carolyn was still hanging around with all these recruit guys so maybe it was time to go to some of her parties.

My faith was terribly neglected during the years of working and university. Time available resulted in trying to fit living my life into perspective. I knew that the religious life was not meant for me because there were just too many guys around me all the time. I felt that I wanted to eventually marry and have a family of my own. I craved someone to really love me for myself, who was meant to be for me. I always remembered to pray at night and continued to ask God to guide me. I had moved in with Jill and was being spoiled with good meals and attention. City transit was my sole means of transportation and the nearest church, St. Peter's, was many blocks away. Occasionally on the weekend, while Jill and Ted drove over to do laundry at Regent Park, I would walk to Mass from there. Weekends were used for university class assignments, doing laundry and some shopping, plus I had a very busy social life.

Carolyn was including me in her social group of friends even though we no longer lived together. Every weekend she had some party happening, with invited recruits at her apartment. Once again, I met another recruit named Richard. I still did not want to ever be serious about marrying a member of the police force. Plus, I could never find anybody that would be as special as Gregg was. Richard was very nice though and we began dating. He invited me to his brother's wedding in Assiniboia. The weekend was wonderful. Richard's relations kept telling us how perfect we looked together. They hoped that they would get to meet me again. The people were all very kind and I had fun. I wasn't serious about Richard and really didn't feel that he was someone I wanted to continue dating. It was sort of cruel the constant way that I continued to avoid him. I knew that he wasn't right for me. He commented one evening about the way that I dried dishes. I became quite angry about this, even though he hadn't said it to be hurtful. Little things that he would do unintentionally were irritating to me. He invited me to his graduation and I turned him down, so he asked someone else. I finally told him that I wanted to stop dating. Hopefully, I desired to spend more time on my university classes. My grades were still not great because I didn't have much time to spend studying and researching.

Overall, the second year of university was very tough as well. Besides my busy schedule, with working on the cleaning staff in the Education building and taking classes, my student teaching left me tired and depressed. I felt like maybe teaching wasn't for me. My first student teaching experience was a disaster. It occurred in the fall of the first semester. I was very unbalanced with everything that I was trying to do. I was placed between two grade one classrooms at Regent Park School. The two teachers were wonderful to me. They were patient and kind. The problem was that being in two classrooms was confusing me. I was trying to overcome my fear of speaking in front of people. The first time that I was to teach a simple lesson, I was nervous beyond words. The teachers were reassuring but I couldn't seem to get comfortable with the children and the workload. I had to rush off from the school, catch the city transit to the university, and begin my night cleaning job. Needless to say, I was getting extremely tired and not enjoying any of this time. After I would get to Jill's house from the cleaning job, I would have to plan lessons, and prepare to teach the next day. I began to hate everything and just wanted to sleep and be left alone.

God stepped into my life once again. I completed the first semester of the second year, debt free. I didn't do great on my student teaching, but didn't fail it either. My Education professor seemed to know that I was working and trying to do too many things. He said that when I went student teaching in the spring semester, it had to be out of Regina and I would have to take some time off from my job. I arranged to take my earned vacation for May, when I would have to leave. I was sent to teach at St. Mary's School in Yorkton. This time, the experience was wonderful beyond words. It was a classroom of grade three students and I was learning with a partner. Barbara, who was fired from Regina Beach and driven to Regina with me that morning, was going to be in Yorkton. Life brought a comfortable, familiar face to work with. The classroom teacher knew how to work with us and I flourished. There was no time that I was even faintly nervous. I was having fun with the children and loved every moment. There were even afternoons when the classroom teacher didn't show up immediately, and I felt comfortable taking over the class. My final evaluation was great and my self-confidence returned.

Upon returning to Regina, I decided to find my own residence again. I was now working with a steady half-time job. I had a couple of classes that I needed to repeat, but I would get my teaching certificate when they were completed. My average was still, barely high enough. I liked Jill, but felt that I was never there enough with her to meet her needs. Her husband was finished his year of teaching and was planning to move back to Regina full time. I quickly found a small, light housekeeping room on Lorne Street and planned to move immediately. Moving would be easy because all my clothes would fit in one suitcase. My other worldly possessions fit in my one round washing bowl.

One afternoon, while I was packing my belongings at Jill's house, the phone rang. When I picked up the receiver, the voice on the other end was very difficult to understand. It sounded like an unusual, sort of African accent. Listening closely, I managed to learn that, unaware to me, a student from Africa actually was studying at the University of Regina. He had been observing me working in the evenings and was interested in me. His strange request was for me to return to Africa with him the next day. He was wondering if he sent his driver for me, would I be willing to go with him and become his wife. He would give me until five o'clock and then he would phone again for my answer. I found this whole event very frightening. I could not even picture this person in my mind, not even to think of marrying him. He did give me his name, where he knew me from, and stated that in his country, he was a royal prince. Meanwhile, Jill came home and I told her the whole story. She knew of him from her work at the university. Jill made some phone calls and validated all of his information. The decision was mine to make. When I remember back to this day, it is still hard to grasp. Once again, I could have vanished to Africa, or wherever, and had my family not know what had become of me. I don't even want to imagine what I would have ended up doing or where I would have gone. When the prince called back, I turned down his invitation. He made it clear that I would not get a second chance because he had to leave immediately. I said, "thank you for thinking so highly of me, but this offer is not a good one for me to take."

This chapter included many of the parties, people and positive choices that I made. There were also many mistakes that I had to learn from during this time of my life. My greatest fears remained between God and me. Without his guidance, my whole life and future would have been changed forever. He had a plan for me that I did not know of but trusted in Him whenever things did not feel right. God's grace eventually brought me to the life that I am living in happiness today. He did not ask me to pay a heavy price for any mistakes and failures. God took the lead in my life, maybe because I always asked Him to. He allowed me to learn from failure without dire consequences. Without God's grace my life could have turned out much different. He had a purpose for me, but finding it involved a very rocky road. Without His love and help, I could have never achieved the life that I have now. Hopefully, I am returning some of what His expectations are. I keep taking small steps and hope that I'm going in the right direction.

CHAPTER 4:

my first real love

Life felt good being back on Lorne Street. I was again returning to where I had started living on my own. This time though, I had my own room, with no roommates. The location gave me great access to downtown, which I really missed when I had moved in with Jill. The room was tiny and didn't even have a fridge and stove, but it was all mine. I did have one cupboard, a closet, a hotplate, and a sofa that folded into a small, narrow bed. The refrigerator was just outside the door, in the hallway, to be shared with several other girls.

I wanted another new beginning to improve on my past mistakes. Maybe the excitement of all that dating and activity could sound appealing to most young girls, but I was getting very tired of the attention. I really wanted to be left alone for a while and learn about myself as a person. Some quiet and solitude, with peace and meditation were what I craved most of all. I had been so preoccupied with learning and survival, that I had lost focus and direction. I no longer knew what I really wanted or where I was going. I was unhappy and disoriented but knew that I had survived to this point in my independent life with

God's help. The guilt from the choices and mistakes was horrible. All relationships involve feelings, both mine and the other persons. I knew that I had been hurtful in some of the relationships, yet my feelings had been hurt as well. I also felt that I had been deceitful and did not want to face God in some of the things that I had done. I felt a sense of worthlessness. I eventually made myself believe that with so many people in the world God wasn't even paying attention to me. He has much more important things to worry about than one person. Maybe I should walk away from thinking about God and all this guilt and move into living for myself the best that I can.

That summer holiday, after returning from Yorkton, was still very active, contrary to my deepest desire for introspective thought. Past relationships kept returning. At this time, Doug, the guy from high school, showed up one evening while I was out with friends. I knew for sure after that encounter that he no longer mattered to me. Jim still stopped by occasionally and I knew that friendship was all we would ever have. There were several other instances of recruit parties with Carolyn but I never allowed any real interest there. There was even some guy that I had met while I was out with a few friends. He made me promise that I would await his return from a trip to British Columbia. It just seemed that I had all these men in my life and none of them seriously mattered to me. I felt sure that they would make someone a suitable husband. I really never even mentioned all the people that were gravitating through this point in my life. They weren't right for me. I was tired of the guilt. Was the choice that I just made right or wrong? I resigned myself to the fact that I could go into adult life alone. I had to complete my last remaining university classes, bring up my grade average, and proceed to find a better job than working on the cleaning staff. My mind was made up.

Whenever I am totally resigned that something will never happen in my life, it happens. That is exactly what takes place constantly and happened in this case as well. The fact that I was totally committed to pursuing a single life ironically got turned around. I had been ignoring Carolyn and her recruit parties. That didn't appear to stop her from keeping in touch with me. I mentioned earlier that I had promised, tongue in cheek, a young guy that I would await his return from British Columbia on a Saturday morning. After he left me, the telephone rang and it was Carolyn. She was driving out to the lake on Sunday afternoon with some new friends that she had made. She promised me that these guys were not recruits. Carolyn was determined that I was to meet this guy named Terry, who she believed would be just perfect for me. She would be going with Evan. Seeing as I had been brushing her off for some time and she was so persistent, I agreed to go.

Sunday afternoon arrived and I was not looking forward to it. The last thing I was interested in was meeting some guy on a blind date. Our boarding house, of all single girls, was mostly empty for a beautiful August day. Everyone was out and had things to do. I was stuck waiting for somebody that I didn't have a clue what he looked like. I was getting restless and decided to check on the girl that lived next door to me. Since both of our doorways faced the stairs, I would be able to see who was coming up. Marie was home and offered to make me a cup of tea. We began chatting and enjoying our tea to pass the early afternoon. When Marie heard footsteps ascending the stairs, she stuck her head out the door. The male voice asked if there was someone named Pat who lived on that floor. Marie said, "Yes," and invited him in. I sort of glanced over and said that we should leave. I wasn't interested in a first impression but he seemed all right.

Here we are, two strangers trying to think of something to talk about. Carolyn said that she would be with Terry and Evan to introduce us, but she didn't show up and we were alone. I imagine we were both sizing each other up and making an attempt at polite conversation. I learned that we were driving to Terry's parent's house on Derby Street where we were meeting the rest of the group. My first thought was, "is this guy really still living at home with mom and dad? I'm twenty years old and have lived alone and supported myself since I was eighteen. I doubt that this is going to work." I did meet Terry's family immediately, so that was one problem out of the way, I guess.

We all piled into two cars and headed out of town. Terry did have a great car. It was a 1964 Chevelle Malibu Super Sport, two-door hardtop. The colour was metallic green with white racing stripes. The car had "mag" wheels, with dual chrome exhausts, which was pretty hot stuff at that time. As he rolled out onto the highway, I learned, and was impressed that he had just finished a Bachelor of Arts degree at Notre Dame College, Wilcox, Saskatchewan. I really didn't know about the school but learned that we had crossed paths in Melville. I had been in grade eleven and ushered a performance of the Notre Dame Choral, while Terry had been in the band. He explained that he played the drums in his dad's band, which I found a little hard to believe, since I had heard that line before. Terry had just finished a summer job for the Department of Highways and had returned to Regina for more permanent employment. Meanwhile, he was now working at his dad's frame and wheel alignment business. It was called Bee Line Frame and Wheel Alignment. His dad had an old time band called 'The North Americans'. Terry earned money playing in his dad's band on the weekends. Apparently, they were very busy and he was the drummer in the group.

While driving along, the car driven by Terry's friend, Daryl, pulled up beside us. Daryl started shouting back and forth between the two cars. His car was not bad but really nothing compared to Terry's. Daryl yelled out his window. "Let's race!" My heart stopped beating at that moment. What was Terry going to do? He started to speed up. I could feel my body turning ice cold and starting to shake. "Please, don't race with him. Let him go." I pleaded. Terry glanced over at me and started slowing his vehicle. He didn't even ask why, but just did it. Terry and I both knew that he would have easily won the drag race down the highway. I really didn't have anything to prove and I guess neither did he. That was when I first realized that this guy was pretty special. I then explained to him that I had been in a car accident and told him of what had happened after. He was great and caring.

Our conversation turned to other topics as we let Daryl's car speed ahead. I told Terry that I was able to swim. He told me that he had his

Lifeguard papers. Terry was good at sports as well and it seemed to me at so many different things. I pretended to be good at things, but he didn't need to know that. When we got to the lake, everyone changed into their swimwear. Terry wanted to spend time alone with me further out in the water. He prompted me to swim out with him. I had to admit that I wasn't a very good swimmer, but he only encouraged a fun conversation. He was just kind, sweet, caring, considerate, and easy to talk to. I found myself liking to be around him. I felt very comfortable with him and really didn't know why. The afternoon went quickly and the other girls told me that they thought Terry liked me. I was glad but mostly indifferent at that point. On the way back to Regina, he asked me to go to the drive-in that night. I agreed and that was our first date.

At the end of the first evening, Terry asked if he could see me again. I agreed that he could stop by the university after my cleaning job, and give me a ride home. When my evening shift was over, I did not see Terry's car waiting outside. I usually got a ride with Jackie to College Avenue and then I could walk the rest of the way. It helped me save on bus fare. I didn't know whether Terry was sincere in meeting me or not, so I proceeded to leave with Jackie. Terry finally came to my place later on after some confusion as to where we were actually planning to meet. Following that first mix-up, Terry stopped at the university to pick me up from work every night. He would then take me to Burger Baron for a Super Burger, fries, and a chocolate milkshake. Considering that I could hardly afford to feed myself, his help was very welcome and I looked forward to it. In fact, we enjoyed seeing each other every day. His parents started wanting to discourage him from seeing me, because they felt that we would get tired of each other and he was wasting his money on me. I guess neither one of us took their advice too seriously because we never got tired of each other. The more time we spent together, the more time we wanted to spend together. As I look back over the years we've known each other, we never, ever did get tired of spending endless time together. We still feel exactly the very same way.

Terry was honest with me from the very first. Everything that he told me was truthful. He actually was a drummer that played in his dad's band, unlike the previous two encounters, of which I was never quite sure. Terry did have a degree from Notre Dame, because I met some of his friends from his graduating class. He also had more friends from high school and other places, than I ever dreamed of. There always seemed to be a large group of guy friends around him.

I met Terry on August 8th, just before starting back to finish my last university classes. At first, he thought that he might take some university classes as well and come with me. Terry eventually changed his mind when he discovered that the University of Regina would not recognize his degree from Notre Dame, which was affiliated with the University of Ottawa. During the first couple of weeks of classes, Terry introduced me to the guys. He had a whole gang of high school friends who were studying at the university, but none of them had girlfriends. I soon discovered that I was to be the lone female with the guys for that year at university. It was cool to sit around the tables and feel comfortable playing bridge with the guys. We would be drinking coffee, smoking cigarettes, talking about classes and discussing politics. It seemed that the teams always needed a fourth player and I was it. My favourite game happened one time when the guys needed me as a fourth but none of them wanted me as a partner. So, Harold, who was the lone married student of the bunch, agreed that I could be his partner. I was lucky enough to have the cards to bid a seven, no trump. Harold doubled and we redoubled. I had every face card from the deck in that hand and we had a grand win that day. Years later, I still like to joke about that win when I see the guys. It is one of those once in a lifetime things.

Terry's friends took care of me that year and it was great. I always had someone to sit with and talk to. There was help with my university classes and a ride to school every morning. Terry would always pick me up at the end of the day after my cleaning job. I managed to finish my teaching certificate but did not feel prepared to do a teaching job. There was no need to seek employment since I was already working at the university and could request a transfer to another position. I was encouraged to try for a Library Assistant I position and was accepted.

The university was a great place to work. It also offered great benefits and some notoriety.

One Christmas, our first one to be exact, Terry and I wanted to find a way to spend it together. I wanted to go out to the farm and spend some time with my parents, but I couldn't really afford the bus fare. Terry wanted to drive me to Melville and meet my parents as well. Terry's parents had other ideas. They wanted him to be only with them and not with me at all. They had Christmas traditions that were ingrained in the family from many years back and they all involved his mother and her elders. First the family would go to the grandmother's home; the great-aunt's and so forth until they finally arrived at his parent's house. There was food and presents at every house, all evening long. Their plans did not include me at all. Unfortunately, I spent Christmas Eve and Christmas day alone feeling very lonely. On Boxing Day, Terry finally escaped his family. He came to my one room suite and had his Christmas present for me. It was a new winter coat. It was the most beautiful coat that I could have ever imagined. The coat was a tan colour, with a small fur collar. It was made of wool with a smart, snug fit around the waist. He had an awesome taste in women's clothing. The coat looked great on me and I loved wearing it. Terry said that he noticed that my winter coat looked worn and not very warm. His family was upset that he spent his money on a coat for me. The more Terry's family tried to convince him that I wasn't right for him, the closer we became.

We drove out to my parent's farm near Melville that afternoon and planned to stay overnight. I was concerned that Terry would find the farm too rustic and be offended. I had no need to worry because he was comfortable and well-mannered no matter where he was. Terry was truly one of a kind guy. He was never pretentious or rude. He was always thoughtful and considerate of others. There was never a moment when I felt uncomfortable about something that he did or said. He had a special way with people and I knew it. How could you not grow to care for someone like this? The feelings of liking him were growing and never did a moment produce doubt. This was the guy that God had intended for me. The feeling of being together cannot be described. I knew that he was the right person for me and never needed to second guess or worry about it.

Another incident that attempted to pull us apart happened one evening while we were still dating. Terry's mom and dad had invited me for supper so I was at their home. They had plans with another couple on this particular Saturday night. Terry had a younger brother who tended to get dumped on the great-grandmother and great-aunt whenever his parents made social plans with friends. On this occasion, Terry and I were supposed to take his brother, Trent, to their home. Trent did not want to go over there in the worst way and was crying and fussing. Terry felt horrible about having to do this. The problem was that we were to meet some friends of mine from the university at the Plains hotel lounge. We couldn't bring his little brother in with us, nor could we just walk away and leave him in the car. Terry didn't want to ruin the evening so he insisted on staying in the car outside with his little brother, while I socialized with the group of people. Of course, they noticed immediately that I was alone. After some time had passed, we decided to go over to someone's house. I was uncomfortable about what to do next. One of the single guys was pressing me to leave with him, which would just leave Terry sitting there waiting. I thought that was the cruelest idea that anybody would ever think of. I left the group and told them to party without me. I returned to Terry and unfortunately spent the rest of the night babysitting his little brother.

A terrifying incident in our relationship occurred when Terry had his car accident. He could have easily been killed that night. Terry had just dropped me off at my apartment after a wonderful evening of just driving around and talking. He was on his way home. Terry stopped at an intersection that had an amber light that was flashing. There was a driver speeding into the intersection. The other driver had a red light that was flashing but failed to stop. He crashed into the car that Terry was driving and turned it sideways. He hit the driver's door. Lucky that Terry was driving a big, old '98 Olds that was very large and heavy. He had many serious injuries and went to hospital by ambulance. Terry's younger sister, Trina, phoned informing me that he was in hospital but would recover. She said that she had been out with friends and came upon the accident shortly after it happened. The first thing that she noticed was Terry's drums scattered all over the street. She commented that those drums looked like the ones that belonged to her brother. She watched the ambulance leave and then went to phone me.

Terry and I knew that we had fallen in love. We didn't want or need any more people or relationships. We only and always wanted to be together. I did not have any concerns or doubts. I always knew that I could trust him and to me trust and honesty are extremely important. The time we spent together seemed to go by too quickly and felt like magic. If anything, we tend to pass time with too much humour and constantly joke around. We kind of read each other's thoughts and laugh about the strangest and silliest things. There is nobody like this man and to me he is the absolute best. God knows what he is doing. We totally complement each other's personality.

As time passed, Terry and I decided that we wanted to get engaged and then married. For someone who had all these men in her life, it was weird how badly I now wanted to get engaged and want to spend my life with only one man. I was finished my education for the time being, with a certificate in Education. The new library position was interesting and rewarding. I was once again meeting a new staff of people, with whom I was enjoying working with. Terry already had his Bachelor of Arts degree and was working at his father's business.

The working arrangement between Terry and his father was not great. Every day that I would see Terry after work, he was miserable about the arguments that he was having with his father. His father was an alcoholic, but being the owner of a business and very popular socially, would not admit to it. After work each day, many business acquaintances would stop by and they would spend several hours consuming alcohol. They dangerously made their way home when the drinks were all gone. Terry appeared to be the brunt of conversation. His father liked to air his faults and grievances to these people at Terry's expense. Terry was usually terribly unhappy when he left work for the day. He decided that going into his father's business was not an option.

Terry and I wanted to get married. We were both employed, but just making enough money from each pay check to survive the month. We couldn't dream about the possibility of an engagement ring. It was much too expensive. One beautiful evening in June, after we had been dating almost a year, Terry parked his car outside my apartment. I was still living at the same address, but had moved to a two-room suite. He pulled out a box of Lucky Elephant popcorn from beside the car seat. I watched him with interest. What was he doing? Terry handed me the box of popcorn with a serious look in his eye. I graciously told him that I do not like that type of popcorn. He encouraged me to try some anyway. I insisted that the stuff is terrible. Terry continued by stating how popcorn of that type always has a prize in the bottom. I tell him that you only find junk in them. He prompts me to turn the box upside down and see what there is for a prize anyway. Finally, I agreed, as long as I didn't have to eat any of the popcorn. When I opened the box from the bottom, I found a small box. Inside the box was a beautiful, but simple, engagement ring. It was perfect and delicate. Terry knows that I love yellow gold and want a simple pattern. I happily say, "Yes", when he asks me to marry him. We are now officially engaged and don't hesitate to tell everybody. I couldn't help but wonder how he managed to get the money for such a large purchase. Apparently, Terry's grandmother lent him the money until he could slowly pay her back.

I noticed that there was a job posting for a library assistant and the university was a great employer. I told Terry about the position. He decided to apply for it. Terry went for an interview and was accepted. Terry and I both became employed at the University of Regina and found it much easier getting to and from work each day. We both had much in common with a new group of friends. Terry was happy with his work of shelving library books. Because he already had a degree, Terry soon got a promotion, but still was doing the same work with more responsibility. We decided to keep our engagement a secret for the first while. Eventually we told everyone about our upcoming wedding and they were happy for us. During this time of working together, Terry and I enjoyed weekly social events with the many new friends that we had made. We were really having a great time.

Terry and I had a beautiful wedding on June 9th, 1973 with family and friends. It was a perfect, sunny day, not too hot and not too cold. Looking back in time, I wish we would have had a Mass, but we were not really true practicing Catholics. I really never felt or recognized the difference of having a Mass or not at that time. Father John Colette met with us at St. Peter's Church and asked the many important questions. In that time period, the couple only visited the priest for one short meeting prior to the wedding. We promised Father Colette that we would start attending Mass on Sundays. We weren't avoiding belonging to our church and faith. Church just didn't seem to fit into our lives and nobody seemed interested in turning us in the right direction. It was hard to organize our weekends with Terry being in an old-time weekend band. Quite often, he would be playing for events in small towns and not return home until Sunday afternoon. I did not have my driver's license and depended on a ride to get to church. We were both delighted that the exchange of vows was very short since we only started the wedding at five o'clock in the afternoon. We never had any pre-marriage courses or preparation before the wedding. I only needed to know that I was happy being with Terry. It felt perfectly right. Afterwards, as a young couple, we just figured things out as the marriage days passed. I had already lived alone for several years and felt pretty independent. Truly though, I was not prepared for what I was beginning.

One thing that was troubling me at that time was telling Terry that I needed to kneel beside my bed and pray to God every night. I was afraid that he would think it strange and not want me to continue. I had done this for so many years that it was a part of my life. I could not go to bed and sleep if I did not talk to God. God helped me to move in to the next day. God gave me the strength and desire to live the life that He had given me. I hoped that Terry would understand and not ask me to stop. Of course, I had no need to be afraid. He was very understanding and said that he prayed every night too.

I was unbelievably excited that after our wedding dance, I would be going on a honeymoon. We had saved enough money for a short holiday. Living on the farm did not allow for holidays. There was livestock to be cared for and chores to be done. Farm life was very structured and limited. My honeymoon would be my first holiday ever. We wanted to travel to the Black Hills but all of Terry's uncles insisted that there was a terrible gas shortage and we would run into big problems by traveling to the United States. Terry and I changed our original plans and ended up staying in Canada.

Our first stop was in Medicine Hat. For this farm girl, the driving seemed to never end. I was not used to sitting for so long. The trip was actually quite frightening since that was the farthest I had ever been from home. Terry was an excellent driver and I had no concerns about that. Sitting in the car in quiet thought, brought new concerns to the surface. I was finally fully realizing that I was a married woman. I did not have the freedom that I was used to. It was nice having a partner, but I was no longer able to do as I pleased, whenever I pleased. My life had new responsibilities and they frightened me. While in Calgary, the following day, I decided that everything was too overwhelming for me. I would take my new life situation one day at a time. My solution was to stay married for one year and if that didn't work, I would get a divorce at that time. I did not ever mention this to Terry until years later and now we both delight in the silly thought of it. Next, we proceeded to Banff and Jasper, etc. in the days to come.

While on our holiday in Banff, one morning Terry and I decided to take a scenic trail along a walking path. I was still quite a risk taker and unaware of many dangers in my youth. I noticed a sign warning us to stay with groups of people while walking along the trails. People were everywhere in large groups at first. The groups seemed to thin out with fewer and fewer people as the morning proceeded. I never paid much attention. My thoughts were on excitement, fresh air and adventure. Terry gently reminded me that there could be bears awakening from winter hibernation while we sauntered along trails that were becoming more isolated. I still never paid him much attention, feeling safe and content merely being on a marked trail. At one point, Terry stopped to take a photo of some distant, breathtaking scenery. There was a wooden barricade barring a steep, sharp drop. Terry took the photo, but while balancing his belongings, the leather camera case fell to the ground. It slid part way down the hill and settled slightly out of reach. I became concerned when he insisted on going after it. The risk did not seem the worth of a camera cover. Slowly, Terry reached until he got the item that he sought. The fear of the moment made me realize that we were in other danger as well. Quickly, we increased our pace until we were once again back with the regular population. Terry and I both agreed that more caution was in order for the rest of our vacation.

Arriving back home in Regina, we stayed at Terry's parent's home for a couple of weeks. Our new house was still not completed. It was located on Trudelle Crescent in Normanview West. The house would consist of a kitchen, living room, one bathroom, and three bedrooms covering 850 square feet. It did not come with closet doors, any basement work, landscaping, or a garage. We had to complete all the finishing on our own. We didn't have money for the projects but our parents helped with as much as they could. Eventually, we had a pretty neat looking place. During these early years, we visited occasionally with our neighbours but didn't seem to have much in common. I was still working at the University of Regina library and the neighbour ladies were stay at home mothers. While I was at work, they would gather at someone's house with their children, drink coffee, smoke cigarettes and gossip about any news. Even years later, when I stayed at home with my children, I never found this socializing very appealing.

The first furnishings in our new house came from various family members. We had a variety of furniture pieces that didn't match at all. They had that unique, antique look. I didn't like the style of the modern 1950's look but had to make due with what was given until we could eventually afford our own. We had many new wedding presents that helped decorate and make our house feel truly like our own home.

We were given all the usual necessary items such as dishes, pots and pans, toasters, tea kettles, sheets and pillow cases, blankets, and much more that I won't continue to list. Terry's grandmother on his father's side was very religious. She was blind most of her life and would make people transport her to the cathedral in Gravelbourg every day. People thought of her as being very strange for having this wish. Who would want to go to a church building every day? What would you do there? It was enough to go to church on Sunday. I guess the reason is that she is old. Grandmother Schüssler gave us a crucifix that could hold holy water and candles. It would be valuable if the time came to give someone the last rites, or better known as the sacrament of the sick. I liked the crucifix but it was only another wedding present at the time. Now, as I gaze at this beautiful wooden object, I can feel its true meaning. This crucifix has followed me my whole married life. It is where I have gazed in love, joy, and much sadness. It is where I talk to God every day, when my head is bowed in prayer. It has collected the shine of my many tears of life over the years. This crucifix is a summation of my faith and true love for God. I originally saw a beautiful piece of wood and metal but grandmother saw much more in it than I ever could. Of all our wedding presents, every year it becomes the one most treasured.

Shortly after our wedding, my parents decided to sell the farm and move to Regina. My cousin bought the property, including the land and buildings. Maybe this would be silly to another person, but what I am about to mention is very special to me. When I was born and began my life on the farm, we already had a beautiful, mongrel dog named 'Sporty'. Sporty was just a puppy, but went everywhere that we went. We played with him and the other dogs every day. Sporty would never bite us. He would occasionally growl if we got too rough with him. When we would leave the farm, Sporty was there to stand guard. He always kept skunks, strange dogs, porcupines, or any other unwanted animals out of the yard. Sporty was always the leader and never harmed cats or children. When we arrived back home, Sporty was there to welcome us with a friendly bark and hug. Everybody loved

Sporty and he was part of our family. That dog lived on the farm, the whole time that our family did. What would become of Sporty when the farm was sold? He was now very old in dog years but we hurt with the idea of leaving him behind. My cousin offered to come every day, feed our dog and check on him. Sadly, Sporty knew what was happening. After the farm auction, there were still a few last minute details to look after before the final move. A few days before my parents moved away, they went out and discovered that Sporty had died overnight. Sporty was not being left behind. He had done a great job and been part of a family. With that much love earned, Sporty was now in heaven with God.

Following my car accident, there was still some hospital time ahead for me. The doctor's had decided to do some reconstructive surgery on my nose since most of the cartilage had been removed. This is the third time that I would be going through the glamorous black eyes, with a white cast and tape covering my face. It was also the time that Terry decided that I should meet Pere Murray and take a trip to Notre Dame. I remember it as a once in a lifetime wonderful afternoon. I liked Pere Murray the moment that I met him. Terry and Pere immediately began talking about the past and how Terry was always there to drive him to class in the morning. He offered us a drink in a shot glass as we sat in his comfortably cluttered office. He had a scattered mess everywhere and everything was covered in cigarette ashes. Pere was extremely interesting and talked to us about a variety of highly educational topics. He recited by memory from a book that he handed over to us. Not even once did he mention my nose cast or refer to it, even though I felt very self-conscious. When our visit was complete, Pere suggested that Terry take me to the archives that hold his rare book collection. Jokingly, Terry commented that all the years that he went to the college, Pere never allowed him in the room and I get invited in only one afternoon visit. That particular day is now engraved in my memory as a golden opportunity to have met one of the great people of our time. There would be many more visits to the college because of Terry's musical connection to the choral, but none would ever be as special as that day was.

One of the final upgrades to my life during this period before having children was to learn to drive and hopefully get my driver's license. Terry had made a few attempts at instructing me in the art of automobile control and I had made some progress. He wanted me to begin driver training because Terry felt more comfortable with me learning in a Driver Training car. I still had my learner's license from before my car accident but didn't want to drive any more. My dad had tried to coax me to drive a couple of times while still on the farm but I really didn't ever want the responsibility again. I finally agreed to the lessons after Terry's consistent encouragement. I took driver training around the city and actually became quite good at it. The driver trainer, who Terry knew as a fellow musician, decided eventually that I was at the point to take my driver test for my operator's license.

The morning of my driver test was very strange. It was a snowy day in early December. Ernie, my driver trainer, suggested that we go out driving before my test. He felt that I would be less nervous after doing some driving around first. Ernie came with the driver training car to my house. He cautioned me because the streets were quite icy and people were on their way to work. I slid in behind the wheel, actually feeling quite confident at the time. He wanted me to practice driving downtown through the one-way streets that can be quite tricky. As we came to an intersection, Ernie told me to pull over and park the car against the curb because he felt that an approaching vehicle would not be able to stop on the icy slope. He was right because the other vehicle was traveling much too fast. I pulled over and parked as he asked but the other driver saw me at the last minute. He decided to try and stop but was unable, so he cranked the wheel and ended up skidding into the front of the driver training car. Ernie had to get the accident information while I waited. I knew that this incident was not my fault. It was unsettling that the front of the driver training car was smashed and looked quite horrible. It was also time for the driver test. When I arrived at the building, I had to fill out an accident report. I was then taken for my driver test in the smashed car. I was quite calm with the feeling that the worst was over and nothing horrible could happen to me any more. I got my driver's license that morning. The next report that I filled out stated that during the accident I had my learner's license, but since then, I had completed my driver's test successfully. I now had my driver's license.

CHAPTER 5:

the schüssler family

A couple of years into our marriage, Terry and I decided that we would like to start a family. Little children and especially babies never held any fascination for me. Yet, for some reason at this time in my life, having a child became very important. I never enjoyed baby sitting. My thinking became that having our own child would be different. Since you would know the child every day, any problems that the child would have could be solved by us as parents. You wouldn't always seem at a loss as to what to do next.

Within a couple of months, I found that I was with child. For the first early months, I was so terribly ill that only the idea of a baby growing within me made it all feel worthwhile. Each day was a struggle. I felt tired continuously, and never wished to eat. Going to work each day was difficult but I seemed to manage. I never took sick days. Having people around kept me from thinking about the discomfort and feeling sorry for myself. Slowly, the days seemed to creep by and I was led to believe by my doctor that soon I should begin to feel better. I never did get over the morning sickness and could eat very little. Yet, the baby appeared healthy and the doctor seemed satisfied. The realization was amazing that we were going to have a new little person in our home. I was radiant with joy.

Four and a half months into the pregnancy, everything went wrong. One evening, while I was walking downtown with my sister shopping, I began to feel strange. It felt like the baby was just going to fall out of me. There was no pain or discomfort. Things like this shouldn't just happen without a reason. I tried to ignore my feeling that something wasn't right. When I went home and rested, everything seemed better. The next day after work, I knew that something was really wrong and told Terry. He insisted on taking me to the hospital emergency. They admitted me immediately for a specialist's examination. The doctor explained to me what was happening, but I did not want to believe it. I had a special problem but because it was discovered at the hospital, I would never have to experience it again. My only concern was for my unborn child. The doctor sympathetically told me that they would try to save it, but he was doubtful of success. He also said that there was a strong chance that if the baby survived, it would have brain damage. This couldn't be happening to me. Not after all the days of sickness, mixed with happiness, I had just struggled through.

I was filled with terror and dread throughout the night. There was beginning to be discomfort and pain. I wanted this nightmare to be over. The following morning, they took me to surgery. When I was awakened back in the room, I had a horrible feeling of emptiness and loss. The baby did not survive and they could not do anything to save it. I froze inside and refused to allow any feelings. I wasn't going to cry no matter what. While we were walking down the hallway out of the hospital, Terry asked me, "don't you even want to know what the baby was?" I replied, "It was a boy." That was the first time that a prediction had ever come true. The knowing of the past came back to me right then. I realized that something had told me years earlier that this was going to happen. I choose to believe that God, who I strongly believe in, was giving me time to prepare and know my baby before I lost him. Otherwise, I would have missed out on all the special moments and caresses that I can still deeply remember. At the time, I was filled with anger and hatred towards God and the Blessed Mother. They had taken something special from me. The Sunday after being released from the hospital, Terry and his family took me to St. Peter's church. It was difficult to sit through the Mass when I only wanted to go home and cry alone. We went for breakfast but I didn't feel very hungry. Once again, years later, I thank God that they did that because I remembered it always and what a wonderful place to be. I eventually believed that if my past feelings became true, God would give me more children. They would be healthy and strong. I would never have to go through the loss of a child again. I didn't want another baby; I wanted the one that I had just lost. I'm sure that God forgave me my hatred and anger because it was buried deep within the pain. I developed a deeper recognition of God when I began to ask Him for help in dealing with the hurt. That is when God became real to me again. I would see God everywhere and recognize His works in ways that were all too obvious for me to miss.

The wonderful, specialist doctor that I had met at the hospital was supportive and encouraging. He was caring and made me feel confident that everything would be all right. I really liked him. This doctor had a special way of working with people. He said that as soon as I felt better, we should try for another child. That is the last thing that I wanted to think about. I was desperately grieving for our loss. If anyone ever believes that it is just a fetus in there, and not a person created by God, they are unbelievably mistaken. I could never have felt more hurt and pain for what I had just been through. The emptiness was a feeling beyond living a lifetime with someone and thinking you had time to know that person. My son was alive and real to me. Years later, in my heart, he is still a part of our family. I want him to know that he was wanted and loved.

Time passed and we eventually did move on. We still wanted a family and felt that the next child would be a boy as well. One morning, about a year later, when I woke up from a sound sleep, I had been visited in a dream during the night by a dear friend who told me that I was once again pregnant. It was still too early to know from a test, but I knew that I was anyway. I went straight to the specialist doctor when I knew for sure. During this pregnancy, I was just as sick as I was the first time. The doctor would not allow any pills or medications; he made me tough it out. He was fantastic with me and I had the best of care. Because of the early morning sickness, Terry convinced me to stop smoking. Quitting was difficult since I was still working in the university library and at coffee most of the staff smoked. Smoking was not thought of as a health issue in that time period. It was very common for all people to smoke in all locations. I became an exception to this practice at that time. Our son, Shane Patrick was born on October 17th. He was a healthy 8 pounds and 8 ounces. What a beautiful baby he was! Shane was easy to care for and was rarely irritable. I was able to take him anywhere in public without fussing on his part. We were truly blessed.

My favourite part of being pregnant again was that my sister, Geri, offered to help me sew some maternity clothes. I bought the material and some patterns. They were taken to her house. She was very good at doing most things and sewing was just another one of them. Geri and I got to once again spend endless hours visiting and talking about everything. I never got tired of wanting to spend time with her. After completing a large number of beautiful new clothes, I got opportunities to wear them. It was fun to show off our new creations. I wanted Geri and Paul to be Shane's godparents simply because we had such a loving family relationship.

I decided to quit my job at the university and stay home with my son. This was done partly as an excuse to one day pursue my degree in education again. It had always been in the back of my mind and made me restless for enjoying other things. Plus, I wanted to take care of my own family and not drive them to some babysitter every morning. Terry and I knew that this would be tough financially. Terry was well paid for working at the university and made money by playing for dances on the weekend. With all the work, we would have just enough money to pay for our house and vehicle. Every payday, we would purchase most of our groceries and I would make most of the food last for the entire month. Occasionally, we would have to buy extra perishable food items, but didn't add too much else. The time went quickly caring for our son and looking after our home. Neighbour lady coffee and smoking visits never interested me, so I spent most of my time caring for my family. After a year without smoking, I had basically overcome the habit. It was tough having Terry still smoking. One afternoon, we were sitting in our home with some visitors. They were all smoking except for me. The urge to start again was very strong. I told Terry that if he continued smoking, I would start again. That was when he decided to quit and support me. It was harder for him because he was still around people that were habitual smokers. Neither Terry nor I began smoking again. We are glad that we quit the bad habit when we did and prevented many health problems later in our life.

My anger and resentment towards God for my earlier loss kept me from wishing to go to church. In my heart, I still believed that He could have stopped it from happening and was to blame. Terry was busy with his music and as a result we fell away from the church once again. The strange part was that I could miss church without guilt but could never go to bed and sleep without talking to God even if I was angry with Him. He would be told about all my thoughts, problems and hurt, quite openly. The Mass seemed foreign and I felt like a stranger. I did not understand my religion. Years of memorizing catechism statements, proved to be unimportant in my present life. I liked receiving the Holy Eucharist because it made me feel better but the Word was not of interest to me. We were pulled back to church for a while because we wanted to have our child baptized. It was simple. You made an appointment with your parish priest who occasionally saw you attend Mass. I didn't think that the priest noticed if I was there or not anyway. These words truly identify how my world changed when my belief in God turned everything around for me years later.

I got a short library contract during that time. It gave me a little extra income and a chance to associate with adults again as a professional. I liked having the break but knew that I truly wanted to be a mother at home. Having Terry gone so often was not easy. Many times, he would work all week at the university, and when Friday came, he would leave with his father's band. Sometimes he would only be gone overnight, but usually he spent the weekend in the town and came back on Sunday afternoon. The loneliness for adult company and especially being with my husband was terrible most days. Yet, I would not replace those vital years for raising both of my children. I believe that when children are young, we instill in them our values and behaviours for a lifetime. It is a time to be teaching our children about life. We tell them what is acceptable and how to function in our home and society. I did not wish to pass my most important job to some stranger. It was my family and I would be responsible for their care. I would always be there for them no matter what they faced in life.

One Sunday afternoon, we were invited over to Terry's parent's house for supper. When I originally met Terry, there were five generations on his mother's side of the family. He still had a great-grandmother. On this occasion, I was sitting at the kitchen table feeding Shane. I was carrying on a casual conversation with his grandmother. There was just the three of us. She looked directly at me and stated that she would not be living too much longer. I was caught by total surprise as to why she should say this to me. It really bothered me and I felt uncomfortable. The family found some of the things she would say unusual, but she was telling me something much too personal for comfort. I tried to assure her that other family members should be told of her feelings but she would not hear of it. She just looked me in the eye and reaffirmed her comment. Grandmother only wanted me to be privilege to this information. I do not know why, nor have I ever found out. Within a short time, her foretelling came true but I kept it private as she had wished.

Three and a half years after Shane was born, we had a beautiful, healthy daughter, who we named Sharla Terri. She was also a joy to our life and home. Terry and I had her baptized at St. Peter's church by the parish priest one Sunday afternoon. We never had to attend any special classes, just make an appointment and show up. Shane was early to start walking and was into everything as a child. Sharla was the opposite and began talking at an early age. She loved books. Sharla would also spend hours drawing and colouring at the table. We had started Shane in pre-school shortly after Sharla was born. Sharla and I would get out every day to drive him and pick him up. We got to know all the new families and made many friends. When Sharla was two years old, some of the mothers of the community would plan fun afternoons for our children at a leisure center room made available for our use. The early years with my children were enriching and valuable. Getting to church was tough with little children so we seldom attended.

A terrifying event happened while we were still living on Trudelle Crescent. Terry had been shoveling snow late in the afternoon. He started complaining about not feeling well. Shane went to bed with a fever and upset stomach. In the middle of the night, Terry was in so much pain that he decided to drive himself to the hospital. We didn't live very far from the Pasqua hospital, so he felt that he wouldn't disturb family during the night. Terry would not consider phoning for an ambulance. He just got dressed, got in the car and left. Meanwhile, I am now wide awake and worried. Terry said that he would phone me when he arrived at the hospital. Cell phones did not exist. Night turned into morning and I did not hear from him. I was frantic with worry. Meanwhile, Sharla woke up crying, got out of bed and vomited all over the floor. Both children are now sick, my husband has driven to the hospital and I haven't heard from him. My mind was thinking that the worst had happened. The waiting and not knowing was unbearable. As the day wore on, Terry was given a slim opportunity to phone me and I learned that he had been admitted to the cardiac care unit. He had suffered an inflammation of the sack that surrounds the heart. My whole night had been spent in prayer and asking God for help. They were able to help Terry at the hospital and eventually he recovered. The children suffered from stomach flu but recovered from that in a few days as well.

The greatest test of faith came when Sharla was only fourteen months old. We went for a short visit to Greenwater Provincial Park with Terry's family. At the park, log cabins could get rented for periods of time. We rented a two-bedroom cabin for a long weekend. Terry's family was sharing a gorgeous, large two-storey log cabin with a loft. The weather was slightly cold for June but the scenery was rugged and beautiful. Sharla had been suffering with an ear infection when we left home and our family doctor had been treating her with Penicillin. She had used Penicillin in the past with no problems. We were using the last of the drug and Sharla was just about over her infection. Medical people always tell you to use all prescribed medications until complete and empty. That is exactly what I was doing. I started noticing some small red welts on her at the end of our first day. I didn't pay much attention since Sharla had taken the medication for some time. By afternoon of the next day, I noticed that she had developed a major rash. Having more concern by this time, we decided to drive to the medical center at Porcupine Plain and have her checked over. The doctor there thought that she may be allergic to some vegetation in the area. He gave her a shot of anti-allergen medication and she seemed to be improving. I bathed her and put her to bed for the night after another dose of Penicillin. An uneasy feeling was bothering me as I prepared for bed. Thinking that I should trust the doctor Sharla had seen earlier in the day, I said my prayers as I crawled in for my sleep. I asked God to watch over us and especially Sharla.

When we awoke the following morning, I went immediately to check on my little girl. She had been quiet all night so I thought that she had a good sleep. What I found frightened me beyond words. She was not moving at all and her whole body was swollen. When I picked her up in my arms, she would bruise as I touched her. I wanted to leave for Regina at once. Family members suggested that we return to the clinic at Porcupine Plain but I wouldn't consider it. I believed that we would be wasting time and she would die that day. Terry and I packed up our belongings at lightning speed and headed straight for Regina as fast as we could go. As we sped along not even thinking of getting stopped by the Police, Sharla was turning black and blue over her entire body. The only hope was the fact that she continued to breathe. I had faith in my heart. God promised me that He would never take another child from me. I really believed that to be true and prayed all the way back home.

Back in Regina, we quickly phoned the pediatrician that Sharla had been seeing while she was still in the hospital. I was so frantic that they promised the doctor would meet us in emergency. When we arrived at the hospital, the doctor there examined her and affirmed that he did not know what the problem was. He said that we should take her back home and go to our family doctor the next day. I wouldn't leave until the pediatrician examined her as well. When the child specialist saw her he asked me what I felt the problem was. I could only surmise that it was the medicine that she had been taking. He said that I was correct and in fact Penicillin reactions generally begin with the throat constricting. The person chokes to death. He gave Sharla a needle. The swelling and bruising soon began to decrease. If she ever has Penicillin again, Sharla will die immediately. God saved my beautiful girl, I believed and without His promise she would be with us no longer. My faith and belief in God became stronger than ever after this day and I knew that He was watching over us.

Our house on Trudelle Crescent seemed too small and restricting as the children began growing up. It was not close to any parks or play areas. There was not much for the children to do unless I went outside and constantly supervised them. That thinking led us to search for a larger house about ten years after buying the first one. We liked the neighbourhood and didn't wish to move too far away. We soon noticed that a larger house was for sale only a couple of blocks down the next street. It had a great location close to the school and the back yard was connected to a city park. The children could have a large back yard to enjoy and I could also see them playing on the park play structures. We decided that we could afford the move even though I was still not employed and staying home with the children. Unfortunately, this house purchase proved to be a big mistake in our lives.

CHAPTER 6:

back to school

Terry and I bought ourselves a larger house on Bastedo Crescent, just a couple of blocks from where we had always lived. We had chosen a terrible time to move and the years that followed were very tough for us. One of the first things that we realized was that the Real Estate agent, who had been a family acquaintance for years, misled us. She was more loyal to her employer, who was the original owner and was having difficulty selling the property. There were many problems with the house that she had the training to hide from us. The agent made us believe only the selling points of the property but was not honest about the many things that needed repair. Sad to say, we had barely moved in and already were disappointed. We knew that we had landscaping to do because the original owner let all the plants die from neglect before our possession date. With the shrubs dead, you could see that the front step had a large hole in the side and was pulling away from the house. It would have to be replaced. The garage needed mud jacking to straighten the flooring which was slanted. The carpet was dirty and smelling from the dogs that roamed free and there was animal fur covering everything. This just mentions a few things and the list goes on. To add more insult to injury, the interest rates became higher than we expected and our payments would be difficult to manage. We also did not want to live in a house that needed so much repair knowing we would not be able to afford it. Making the repairs would not increase the value of the property either. At that time, we felt trapped. We now needed to make the best of our poor choice.

The following years were like a time of depression for us. Terry didn't get a financial increase at the university for a few years because the provincial government had frozen wages. The price of everything was continually increasing. We could barely meet all our payments but still seemed to manage. I recall the summer that we couldn't afford to replace the glass globe fixture for the light on the outside of the back door overlooking the patio. It probably only cost a couple of dollars, but every one of our dollars was accounted for. If Terry wasn't playing in a band, we would have gone into debt. Even that became a problem when Terry's dad suffered a heart attack and the band stopped taking bookings. We depended on the extra income so Terry decided to play tape music. He did that for about a year or so. Eventually, Terry got back with a band and that helped somewhat. Our parents helped us to buy the children clothes and items for the house. Every day, it seemed that we would struggle through our needs but the money always came from somewhere to help us. To have a saving's account for enjoyment or a future, was a dream. All our income was used to pay taxes, house payments, car repairs, utilities, groceries and generally just survive. Once a month, we took the luxury of going to McDonald's for a hamburger treat. The strain on our marriage was terrible because it seemed that Terry was always working and we weren't getting any further ahead. He looked very tired and worn out.

About a year after moving, I decided that I wanted to do something to help but was not sure what. Terry had been playing in the new band that he joined when I knew for sure that my help was needed. That Saturday night, he had played for a dance outside the city. The highway had been covered with ice and the driving was treacherous.

The musicians had to return early in the morning. Terry described how horrible the return trip had been. I didn't want my husband killed on some highway late at night when returning from a dance. I realized also that the children were growing up and the day would come when they wouldn't need a stay at home mom. I was restless and needed to do something to further myself. It was great volunteering at the school and community center, but I needed more meaning in my world. I always wanted to be a teacher so I thought about pursuing that. When I mentioned to my parents one evening that I wanted to go back to university, my mom offered to fund my education. She suggested that I could pay her back and not have to worry about paying interest on loans. I knew her offer was too good to turn down. I would begin by taking one class in the fall semester.

After meeting with a counselor, my classes became all set up for a Bachelor of Education degree. I knew exactly which classes I still needed and could work at completing them over time. My major would be in Education Psychology to help me find employment in a needed area. I would also take classes in Education Library since I had already gained experience in that field. My overall average was not very high, which meant that all my future marks would have to be higher than 65% in order to attend convocation. I now had a mission and a goal ahead. I could take one class at night for the first semester. Going to university would get me out of the house. I would spend more time with adults and I would be learning, which I was craving.

At first, just attending university again was stimulating. The idea of what I was doing was making the assignments seem less difficult. I was having a terrible time trying to understand the theory though since it was all new to me. Other people in the class talked about past experience and knowledge. Most of them were already employed as Special Education teachers attending university to meet government employment standards. I didn't understand enough to even converse with them. I didn't know anything about 'exceptionalities'.

Eventually, the first scheduled examination arrived. I had studied hard but feared that I wouldn't do very well. My fears were warranted for I scored horribly. I felt that I was doing something way above my ability level. Doubt paralyzed me at that time and I contemplated cutting my loss and not going any further. I just wasn't intelligent enough for university. I couldn't quit though because it would mean dumping all responsibility back on Terry's shoulders. With much frustration, I did what I always do when everything goes wrong. I knelt beside my bed and cried in prayer. I told God all of my troubles until the tears finally stopped. Deep inside, I knew that I was meant to become a teacher but I didn't see how that was going to happen. Being thoroughly exhausted, I fell asleep.

I decided that I was going to complete my class no matter what the results would be, since I had paid for it. Strangely, the new section of material was more interesting. I began to understand the content, communicate ideas with others, and looked forward to the upcoming classes. When I received my final grade, it was above the 65% that I needed to continue with the program. During the winter semester, I took another Ed. Psych. class and this one was very interesting. I was beginning to achieve and anticipated moving forward. My grades were increasing and the feeling of belonging was immense. Many high level classes allowed me to now demonstrate my newly acquired knowledge. The confidence and interaction were addictive and I couldn't stop any longer, even if I wished. I began to challenge statements in class and offered my own unique ideas. Presentations became commonplace and my fear of speaking in front of others mainly vanished. After the first couple of years, I decided to push for the completion of the program and began taking summer classes. By this time, I was certain that all my grades were high enough and I would graduate from the program in the fall.

A strange coincidence happened during my final class in August. I arrived in the seminar room of the Education building. I looked around and didn't know a single person. Finding only one vacant seat around the table, I decided to occupy it. Smiling, I said "Hi", to the people on each side of me. The person to my right smiled but ignored me; the person to my left seemed quite friendly. I looked in his direction and introduced myself. We exchanged names and began a conversation. I learned that he was taking his final university class, just as I was, and that he was already employed at Notre Dame College in Wilcox, Sask. There was an immediate bond and we had much in common to talk about instantly. I told him about Terry and his musical participation over the years. I learned that he was taking over the choral program at Wilcox that fall. We talked about Pere Murray and the visit Terry and I had with him. Once the professor started the class, we had to stop our visit. Every class after that we sat together. We became friends, very comfortably talking about everything and anything. We still continue to occasionally visit into the present time. Once again, God had connected me with future events that would happen during my teaching career. I was not even close to being employed and had no idea that there would be a future connection.

During the years that I was attending university, my family was growing as well. Shane scared me one early afternoon as I was awaiting his return from Grade one. Because I always met him a block from the house, I was waiting on the main street close to our home. When half an hour passed and I didn't see him coming down the street, I began to panic. We only lived about three city blocks from the school, so I allowed Shane to walk two of them alone. I wanted to begin teaching him some independence. Sharla was in the house alone and I didn't want to leave her for very long. Finally, in desperation, I crossed the busy street and went in search of Shane. Two older girls came walking up to me with Shane between them. Apparently, some grade eight boys had thrown him into a dumpster and closed the lid. I found it hard to believe that older students would treat a little guy so horribly. The girls were passing by, heard him and proceeded to release him from his imprisonment. That was my first encounter with bullying in our young family. I was fortunate to have met his classroom teacher previously. What a fantastic, creative person and mentor she had become to me since I was studying education. Watching her work with the children was extremely inspirational and I learned a lot from her. She resolved to deal with the problem and arrange punishment for the guilty students.

God protected Sharla again when she was in grade one. It was the second time that He had saved her life. We had just finished lunch and I walked to the main busy street with my children. Shane had crossed and was well on his way to school. There were no vehicles approaching so Sharla said good-bye to me and crossed the street. I waved and watched her proceed on her way. On the opposite side of the street, one of her classmates was getting a ride with her grandfather. They stopped to offer Sharla a ride with them. She knew that a ride with strangers was not acceptable. So, Sharla turned around and ran back towards where I was standing to ask for my approval. She didn't see an oncoming car and he didn't see her either. The image was like slow motion. I could see the vehicle screaming to a halt and tires squealing on the pavement. My heart almost stopped in fear at that moment. My memory was of a little girl screaming and crying, with two pigtails flying behind her as she ran. We embraced each other as she reached my side of the street. The almost accident had been mere inches from becoming a disaster.

My sister, Geri and her husband, Paul separated and eventually divorced while I was attending university. Marriage at such a young age, with all the responsibilities of a family, proved too much stress and strain on my sister and brother-in-law's relationship. Geri moved to Saskatoon. She went back to school and finished her education by upgrading. Then, she went on to SIAST to study heavy machine operating. Geri eventually got a job working at the Cominco Potash mine. She met Ken, who worked at the Corey Potash mine; they fell in love; and, got married a few years later.

My faith in God was drawing me once again closer to the church. It was also connecting with my desire to teach, which had become very strong. We had been attending St. Peter's church frequently with Terry's parents. Terry and I, with our family, weren't going every Sunday as we should have been but were attending quite often. Some weekends we believed, were far too busy for church to be added as well but, we mainly attended. Terry and I learned that our son was at the age to receive his First Eucharist. The apparent problem was that Shane wanted to participate with his classmates. The school community in our area belonged to Holy Trinity and we were not parishioners there. Terry and I decided that we should switch churches. We would probably attend more often as a family if the church was closer to our home. So, we registered at Holy Trinity church.

One weekday evening, the doorbell rang unexpectedly, and the parish priest from Holy Trinity was standing on the step. We graciously invited him in to our living room. He declined any refreshments. Terry and I proceeded to inquire as to what prompted this visit. Father told us that he was curious about our reasons for now attending church at Holy Trinity. We felt quite confident, stating how our family needs had changed and we wished for our children to receive their First Eucharist with their classmates. He became quite agitated about what we had said and his voice became loud. The priest was extremely upset that we hadn't switched churches years earlier. We hadn't seen any reason to switch since St. Peter's was the church where we were married and our children were baptized. The reasoning did not sit well with him. Father gave us a severe lecture about having made an immediate change when we moved into the area. Terry and I decided that he wasn't going to upset us or change our minds. We were now going to Holy Trinity and there wasn't anything he could do about it.

Sadly, that priest would make most people not want to attend his church. I needed to get a priest reference for teaching eventually and my children needed to receive their sacraments, so I was adamantly serious about going to Holy Trinity. My mind was made up that from that time onward, we were scheduling Sunday Mass at Holy Trinity into our lives. I felt more comfortable with the age of my children and even if Terry was away playing music for dances, I could drive to the church and manage on my own. If I was able to drive to the university classes, drive to preschool programs, surely I could drive to Holy Trinity on Sunday mornings for Mass. That priest was going to get to know me! In fact, I was planning to find some ways to get involved in the Parish but wasn't quite sure how yet.

Notices were sent to the Catholic families about a special meeting for children in grade two who were planning to receive their First

Eucharist. The meeting was to be held at the church on Sunday afternoon. Since I hadn't seen the need to arrange for babysitting, we were planning to attend as a family. Sharla was three years old and quietly behaved so I did not see any problem. Shane was included in the children who needed to participate at the meeting. Just before two o'clock, we drove to the scheduled meeting. Father was greeting people at the door of the church. When he saw Sharla, he yelled at us to leave. The priest was angry that we had brought her to the church and he insisted that we leave at once. Sharla was not permitted to be present. Terry and I were at a loss as what to do next. I offered to leave for home with Sharla and would drive back to the church later. There were no cell phones at that time, so I would return in a couple of hours. Here was a reason why we could have walked away from the church feeling completely justified, never to return. Church experience was not positive for us at that time. We could have had every excuse to leave. I don't think that way and tend to become stubborn. Yes, I was very angry but nobody was going to tell me to leave from a church. Clergy are supposed to bring people to God, not chase them away. So, with that thought, our family proceeded to attend more events at the church than ever before. In fact, after Shane received his First Eucharist, I registered to volunteer for leading with Children's Liturgy.

The first time I was scheduled to instruct the Children's Liturgy group, I was very nervous. I had never taught such a large group of three year old children before. That area of Regina was growing rapidly with young families. My past teaching was at St. Mary's in Yorkton, but that was now years earlier and the children were older. I had done some planning with the children's group at the community association, but that was just free play and story time. To me, this was different and more official. Yet, when we were finished and the children came back upstairs into the church, I felt great about my experience. I couldn't wait for my next turn. Many of the mothers teaching Children's Liturgy were already teachers in the Regina Catholic School system and unknown to me at the time, became lifelong teaching acquaintances. I continued to volunteer in this way until Sharla received her First

Eucharist as well. In fact, I volunteered to usher and hand out the roses on that Mother's day Sunday. Because I was now attending Mass every week, and getting to know people from the Parish, I loved coming and looked forward to it. Father finally got to know us, and became friendly and pleasant. He gave me a priest reference for my teaching application. This experience started out as a selfish, personal thing, but Our Lord turned it around into something beautiful and meaningful. After I became reacquainted with my faith again, I desired to attend church on Sunday and never stopped.

While all these time consuming events are happening in our lives, I got another of my 'Heart to Mind' messages. This time, I got the strange feeling that we would be traveling to a funeral. I had a dream that I couldn't remember, but it left me with an unsettled feeling all day. It is that bad feeling that you get when you know that something could be wrong but you are not quite sure what it is. The phone call came the next day from my mother informing us that her sister, my aunt, had passed away in Dawson Creek, B.C. For some reason, maybe because my aunt had always spent time with all of us whenever she came to visit, the whole family wanted to make the trip to her funeral. My sister, Geri, was asked to do the eulogy. Geri and I sat down the night we arrived and wrote some beautiful words about our aunt. She delivered those words with confidence and finesse. Everybody told her what a wonderful job she had done. They openly praised her. I never said anything, even though I had written most of it. It didn't matter, and I didn't need to be recognized.

The university classes that I was attending required me to write various types of essays and reports. Writing has always been something I find easy and natural to do. Since I was quite young, I loved to read and write. One particular weekend, my nephew Paul Jr., who was also my godson, was helping his father with some carpet cleaning at our house. He was completing grade eleven and had an assignment to write a fairly lengthy report for his Literature class. Paul asked me to proofread his written paper. I agreed that it would not be a problem. At this time, because I was still completing my Education degree, I really enjoyed working with any person that I could feel was a student for me to practice my teaching skills. As a result, I sat down with Paul Jr. to read his report. I couldn't believe what he had actually written. There were only two short incomplete pages covered with numerous errors. My first response was for him to get an extension on the due date. I followed up by teaching him the Report Writing Process of doing research using various resources, acquiring information, drafting, etc. Paul wouldn't be prepared for further assignments until he learned what I was more than willing to teach him. The next part is awesome because he eventually went on to university, got his degree, studied theology and became a Minister of the church. My pride in his accomplishment is immense. The reason why I wanted to take the time and teach him so desperately can't be explained. I know that Paul is extremely thankful and often mentions in his homily about the connection God created for us. The teaching at that time led him to religious life so that he could serve God. We will always have a special family love and relationship.

With my final class complete, and my average fairly high, I was ready for convocation. Prior to completion, the students were invited to an interview for the two city school systems, but I was told not to expect any employment from them. At the end of summer, Terry noticed an advertisement for a Special Education teacher with our local school system in the newspaper. When he showed it to me, I paid little attention feeling that I would be wasting my time. Terry phoned me later in the morning from the university and asked if I had done a follow up on the job he had pointed out to me. I knew he would be disappointed if I didn't even try, so I felt obligated to phone anyway. When I phoned the School Administrative office, they directed me to one of the superintendents. He suggested that I come down and fill out an application form. They generally need teachers for the substitute list, even if they don't get employed immediately. With a slight feeling of hope, I decided that I would try and see what would happen. I had nothing to lose. When my application was completed a couple of days later and I went to return it, the office manager directed me into an office. Little did I realize that a spontaneous interview was about to take place.

There was no time to be nervous, or become prepared, so I just had to go with it. The superintendent was very friendly, but direct. I felt very comfortable with him and demonstrated my confidence. I told him about all the things that I had done to prepare for teaching. He stated an interest in my abilities and encouraged me to put my name on the substitute list. The list is used for replacing contract teachers when they are sick or away from their classrooms. I would be acquiring a salary and have some employment. To me, this was a dream come true. Even if I only worked a day or two we would have some extra income for our family.

September arrived, along with the new school year. My children were back in class and my husband was at work also. I relaxed with being at home, and the usual household routines. The phone did not ring for me to teach, even though all my arrangements had been made. If I was phoned in for an assignment, a grade eight girl, who lived a few houses from us, would come to our house when I needed her. She went to the same school as my children and would walk and care for them each day. Terry and I had mapped out routes for me to drive to all the different schools in the city. We now had a second vehicle which was a cheap purchase from his aunt. But, the whole month went by and there was no phone call for me to work.

October is the month of Shane's birthday. The weekend that we would be celebrating his birthday, was the weekend of my convocation. Things have a way of all happening at once. The Saturday and Sunday were two busy days of celebrating and family visiting. After all the work involved with the preparation, needless to say, I was tired when everything was finished on Sunday and the last people finally left for the night. I decided to leave the clean-up for Monday morning. You guessed it! The phone rang for my first substitute job. Excitement generates energy. I was sent to a school, on the opposite side of the city from where I lived. As I started the car, and drove onto the street, I realized that my mapped out route wasn't going to work. Of course, there had to be a train blocking the tracks at that time and the traffic was backed up. Using that route would make me late for my first assignment. I made a quick turn in the opposite direction to the Ring Road. I had never driven on the Ring Road before but knew that I had no choice. I was nervous, very excited, and prayed for help and guidance. God smiled on me because my first teaching experience was absolutely wonderful. Everything went perfect and I loved the grade 4/5 class. There were many phone calls after that, some close to home and some further away. I knew that teaching was my true passion because each day I fell more in love with what I was doing. Many of the teachers requested for me to return. I became very busy, while ironically, my daughter was praying for me to not get so much work and stay home with her more often.

I was requested continuously for substitute teaching from the middle of October until April. After the Easter holiday, a Learning Resource teacher who I had substituted for quite often, needed to take a leave until the end of the school year. I was called in to substitute for her one day only. The following day I returned without being released from the assignment. Once again, I came back to the school without being cancelled. This process of just showing up every day continued until I decided that I might as well do all the year-end testing, just in case the teacher didn't return. I was correct in my assessment and completed the entire school year for her.

The following school year, I was once again prepared to be substituting. I was so thrilled to be earning a salary that a contract was not a concern. I knew that I was helping our family and was taking the stress off of Terry to manage our expenses. During all my years of teaching, my pay was put into the family account for Terry to manage. I never doubted how he took care of our finances. I was always aware of our needs and costs but since Terry had always looked after us responsibly, there was no need to change that. All income in our home was managed jointly in a way that worked for us. When the phone rang this time though, I was offered a position as a Teacher-Librarian with 70% of my time at one school and 20% of my time at another school. I accepted my first one year contract. The year of teaching was great and I was accepted by the staff at both schools. Both of my administrators were pleased with the work that I was doing as well. My experience at the university library was a huge asset but the university was based on the Library of Congress system and our school system is based on the Dewey Decimal System. I had some learning to do. I was teaching Library Science with all classrooms in the schools for one hour each week. This included book exchange and doing another activity for the remainder of the class time. The first class that came in for me to teach consisted of 38 grade eight students. They looked tall and intimidating at the time but it was either sink or swim. I decided to swim and took control at once, realizing that if you don't talk and lead, they certainly will. Later in the year, it eventually helped that I had taken Education Library and did some co-operative teaching with the classroom teachers. The students realized that my time with them was beneficial and relevant. The hour in the library was accountable and not considered mere free time.

While teaching with our school system, I had my first opportunity to go on a one-day retreat. I learned that each year teachers are provided one day for growing our faith together. Over the years, I have had it mentioned to me that other school systems don't get such a day. Some people believe that the day isn't used as intended. Every year that I have taught, I have had the privilege to partake in this day and have never seen it abused. Every spiritual encounter that has taken place has provided for learning and growing. I can't speak for others but I have found that it made me closer to the staff and closer to God. Those days are always special and very unique. Some retreats were held at the Retreat house, while others were held at various locations throughout the city. The retreats had priests, deacons or lay people leading them offering various religious topics and were extremely interesting and informative. I have never experienced disappointment after leaving a retreat and have noticed how close the staff had become when they returned to teaching children again.

The completion of that year saw several schools being closed. I would be without a position for the following year because all contract teachers would need to be placed. There were not enough positions available and I had the option of going back to be a substitute teacher. It would seem strange after having a full year of experience with a staff. I received my letter of termination and appreciation. Since I was a new teacher to the system, I was willing to become a substitute teacher again.

CHAPTER 7:

a final move to our new home

I received a termination of contract letter and was prepared to return to substitute teaching. The telephone rang one day in late August as I was having breakfast with my children. I experienced unbelievable surprise as I was offered a one year contract at a school for special needs children in our system. I accepted the position and arranged to meet with the school administrator. Since I was the first teacher to meet with her, I was given a choice of two classrooms. The one classroom would have senior age students, which meant that they were from thirteen to twenty-one years old, and the second classroom would have younger children but with more medical needs. I opted for the older or senior students. There would be three Instructional Assistants in the classroom for assistance. One of the ladies had been working with special needs students for many years, but the other two were younger and fairly new to the system.

Having my own classroom was very exciting and I attempted to prepare the best that I could. I didn't have money to buy fancy borders and decorations so I made most display items by hand. Meeting the other teachers was very exciting as well. They appeared to be a wonderful group to work with. At the Institute day before the students arrived, I met the staff who would be working in my classroom. They seemed like a great bunch. With schedules set up, and preparations ready, I awaited my first group of students. Realizing that they were non-academic, and since I didn't have any past experience with special needs people, I really wasn't sure what to expect.

The first day arrived; the bus pulled up in front of the school, and now was my opportunity to meet the class. There were a few students in wheelchairs and others needed to be watched for various reasons. The highest functioning students of the group were a Down's syndrome boy and girl. These were my new students and I was going to do my best for them. The daily routines were very similar since the facility did not allow for great activity. The morning started with a short assembly, and sometimes a sing along. There was always a short prayer service and announcements. Afterwards, we would practice some personal hygiene skills, such as face washing and tooth brushing. The remainder of the day varied because we would sometimes go grocery shopping with part of the class, and the following day prepare a lunch to be enjoyed by the students. We also folded church bulletins, went walking outdoors for exercise when the weather permitted, read stories, enjoyed music and sing-along time. Excursions were occasionally arranged to places like the City Greenhouse, city swimming pools, and the Science Center. We were limited in some ways because of the fragile health of some students and the transportation of wheelchairs. Overall, the classroom was running quite smoothly and the children appeared to be doing well, or so I thought.

A teacher would be naïve to think that everything is perfect when she is new and working with three other opinionated adults. Apparently, one of the Instructional Assistants, the oldest lady with the most past experience, was attempting to return the classroom to the way it was managed the previous year, without my knowledge. One day after lunch when I walked back into the classroom, she had prearranged a meeting and insisted that I listen while she did the talking. This lady aggressively attacked my more informal, largely compassionate way of teaching. She wanted more structure and less freedom for the student's personal care. I felt angry that she didn't want to allow a young girl to use the bathroom whenever she asked in her motioning way. I felt that anyone being confined to a wheelchair was entitled to simple things that would allow for their happiness, even if it meant extra work for us. I disliked the abrupt way that she worked with the students. At the day's end, I met with our school administrator, who listened and agreed that this behaviour was unacceptable and the lady was removed from my classroom. She was replaced by someone who also had experience and worked wonderfully with everyone.

The remainder of the year went well. I certainly had learned and grown from the past year. If I had been asked to teach another year at the school, I would have accepted. Instead, at the close of the school year, I was expecting to be terminated from the system after feeling that I had caused a problem with the release of the Instructional Assistant and my lack of experience. The superintendent came to the school and offered me a continuing contract. I could choose between staying at this school or return to work as a Teacher-Librarian. The ladies in my classroom insisted that I should return to the regular school program for various reasons. I accepted a position as a full time Teacher-Librarian between two schools. It would mean traveling and working with two complete school staffs. From that year onward, I was permanently employed until my retirement.

Having my first year of full-time employment started Terry thinking that new possibilities existed for us. That fall, he was out one Saturday, and went to check on a new housing development. The house we now lived in needed so much work that we didn't want to do all the renovations. As mentioned earlier, we disliked it soon after moving in and wished for something better. Terry visited a condominium development in the far Southeast end of the city called 'Windsor Park

Estates'. There were no other buildings around it, just farmland. Most of the units were already sold, but Terry learned that a large unit still existed that could be designed to our liking. The sale would be immediate because other people were interested and the homes were selling quickly. When he came back to our house, Terry was ecstatic with excitement and had fallen in love with the place. He wanted me to see the property right away. I went with him and agreed that it was large and beautiful. We would be able to choose the completion of the main floor with the dividing walls not completed. I had never seen Terry want something so badly. Upon checking with the Real Estate agent, we felt that the purchase was possible. They would sell our property and work both ends of the deal. At the same time, the government was offering grant money for home upgrades. When we moved in, the basement could be developed provided we signed the loan papers before midnight. We agreed to the house purchase, with the possession date of January 1, 1990.

Moving into our new home was very exciting. I was frightened at this point because the relocation took place while I still only had a one year contract. My employment was experiencing the problems mentioned earlier and I didn't foresee the future permanent contract. Our house on Bastedo Crescent went for sale on the market, but people were not wishing to purchase it. They were seeing the many faults that were hidden from us. When we eventually did sell the property, many months later than we had wished or anticipated, we took a loss on it. It was a very costly life lesson for us.

The Christmas break that year was a busy time for us to pack all of our belongings. We decided to forget Christmas and focus on the move. The new house would be our Christmas present. Our parents had the Christmas meals, decorations, and presents for the children. Terry and I rented a truck and prepared to move on New Year's Day. We were fortunate that the weather was quite mild for January and there was very little snow. It made moving much easier than we had ever hoped. When we finally moved into our new home at Brookshire Lane, I felt all the stress that had been loaded on me. Terry was dealing with the pressure as well, but I was frightened that my job would not extend into the following year. When looking in the mirror, one evening before bed, I discovered a red dot on my forehead. It didn't seem too bad and I believed that it could be covered with make-up the next morning. When I woke up and got out of bed, I soon realized that during the night my whole forehead was now swollen. During the day, the swelling extended down past my eyes and onto the tops of my cheeks. I looked like the elephant man and became concerned and panicky. Terry took me to the clinic at our medical center. They sent me to a specialist a couple of days later, where I eventually got treated. The doctor put me on some extremely powerful medication which reduced the swelling and healed my face before I had to return to school.

My uncertain feelings harboured around knowing that we were far beyond our level of income. I didn't feel that we belonged in this neighbourhood and I was afraid for our future. The worry and stress were beyond explanation. Yet, I was going to tough it out and pray that the future worked for us. Every night I prayed and this time I needed God to help me more than ever. God knows what He's doing. The move to our dream home fit into a new, strong faith journey that had yet to begin. At the time, it seemed that the whole venture was a mistake and we could lose everything. Once again, we were living on trust, one day at a time.

To make matters worse, we had to relocate our children to a new school half-way through the school year. Shane was in grade seven and Sharla was in grade four. Sharla was positive about the move since there were only three girls in her grade at the previous school. She was excited about making new friends. Shane seemed comfortable with whatever would happen.

Terry and I were soon called in for an interview with Shane's teacher. We learned that he was being bullied and teased. Shane liked to wear sweatpants and they were popular dress at his old school. Apparently, at this end of the city, jeans were the item of clothing to be worn, so we would rectify that problem with some shopping. Shane shut himself into a boxed-in personal space because of the teasing and wouldn't communicate with anybody, so they all stopped talking to him. The teacher wanted that problem dealt with as well. It would take some time though and things changed when a fellow student decided to befriend our son. The classmate was popular and well respected for being athletic. Shane wanted to play sports with his new classmates, but they wouldn't accept him. We were told that Shane created a sports team of girls and competed with them. The girls accepted him and treated him as an equal and friend. Soon, the boys in his class realized what they were missing out on and changed their attitude somewhat.

Sharla's problems were more difficult and we never could really solve them. The terrible time that she experienced at this new school still troubles me to think about until this very day. Sharla is extremely intelligent and bright. She learns quickly, can work with new ideas, and has a fantastic memory. The principal of the school had a daughter and niece in the same classroom. They had the advantage of their father being very important at the school of course. Once they realized that they had competition and were no longer the most intelligent in their class, they proceeded to bully Sharla and make her life miserable. Terry and I learned that the girls in her class had a special clique. One girl was considered the 'queen bee' and whatever she said, the rest had to do. Sharla didn't want to have any part of this, so the girls didn't hesitate to exclude her. At recess, she found a quiet spot away from everybody else and read a book. Sharla told us later that she was happier alone than being bullied by those girls. Eventually, after a couple of years at the school some of the girls realized that Sharla was a wonderful person and she made a couple of friends. She also is talented in art and Sharla used this talent to pass time when not with friends.

We were now in our new home and there would be no turning back. I knew that I had the good news of a teaching contract and felt that we were officially moved. We were now settled in and summer arrived. We had been so busy unpacking and dealing with school problems, that we had no opportunity to meet our new neighbours. The people that lived around us at our last couple of homes were nice, but we didn't really become very close. Terry and I had always been too involved in various things and opportunity wasn't present for visiting with our neighbours. We were going to attempt more effort in that direction.

Terry and I could not envision the greeting that would come from the other condo owners before we even met them. Many of the people that bought the units were more advanced in years. All the units, except for three, were owned by seniors. Four children existed in the whole development, and they were really not too welcome. One of the children was a baby, so that was not too difficult to deal with. The house on the corner had a boy that was in his early teens, and now we moved in with two school-age children. One Saturday morning, the doorbell rang and I went to answer it. I looked out the tiny window, beside the door, and saw three men from the condo association board of directors standing on our step and discussing something that seemed rather important. When I opened the door, the men entered without waiting for an invitation. Terry came to see what was happening. The men stood together, as they stared at us, and informed us that we did not belong in this neighbourhood. They felt that the intent of the development was for older people to live here because the units were bungalow-style. They insisted that it was obvious and we should realize that this wasn't a family development. Families belonged in residential housing and not in condominium developments. Didn't we see that there was no yard space, just the common ground area? We commented back that there was a park beside us and the leisure center had just been constructed for children to play there. Terry and I assured them that our children would not cause any problems and were well behaved. They left by telling us to keep to our space and that they would be watching us.

Living at the other end of the city prompted us to once again switch to a different church. Leaving Holy Trinity was a difficult choice to make because we had become known there and had made friends. Past experience taught us to make the change at once. Catholic people in this side of the city either attended Holy Child or Holy Cross church. My parents and oldest sister's family regularly attended Holy Child Parish. They had a special pattern of visiting and going to church that had been laid out over the years. My parents bought their house in the Glencairn section of Regina because my sister Sharryl lived there and they could spend more time together. We didn't want to interfere in their space, so Terry and I decided to register at Holy Cross church. Shane had received his First Reconciliation at Holy Trinity church before we moved. Sharla received her First Reconciliation at Holy Cross church. I was still struggling with my faith and how it fit into church during the time of this move. The sacrament of Reconciliation was not of much meaning to me since an early age. Typically, it was a time that we were lined up at the Melville Catholic School and forced to participate. Confession was never a really bad experience; I just didn't see the need for it. I celebrated this sacrament when I attended with Sharla and never bothered going again for about twenty years later. I believed that talking to God every day was all that I needed to do. It is well known that God knows everything, so why do I have to tell sins to a priest? This information and line of thinking will fit into the later chapters that I am writing. Both of my children, Shane and Sharla received the sacrament of Confirmation at Holy Cross. I never got involved in any ministries at this church since all my time was taken up with working and family. Strangely, the Schiissler faith journey seemed to be moving to different locations within the city. We attended Mass every Sunday and really liked the parish priest at Holy Cross. Having just completed university and taken a Religious Studies class, I also really enjoyed listening to occasional guest visits from Father Gorski. I had encountered him initially as a guest lecturer at the University. He was amazingly knowledgeable and interesting.

CHAPTER 8:

a family torn apart

The new teaching contract put me at two schools. The school year had just begun and I spent 60% or three days at one school and 40% or two days at the second school looking after the Library program. Our new home was now on the Southeast side of Regina so I drove on the Ring Road every day. I spent the entire day at each school instead of having the days split. Still, I was very busy with my family and career. My sister, Geri had remarried. Her new husband was named Ken and they lived in Saskatoon. Geri's three children had moved into their teen years and were pretty independent. She had the two boys mentioned earlier, Gerald and Paul Jr., and adopted a baby girl, Jolene, just before Shane was born. Ken had two daughters from his previous marriage. My oldest sister, Sharryl, had three girls, with her youngest a year younger than Shane. We had a growing family that all enjoyed spending time with their grandparents. There were many visits and much family time.

A time of struggle for me was trying to reimburse my mother for my education and she was determined not to accept it. It created a problem because I knew my sisters would feel it was unfair that I should receive extra funding, while they didn't. I believed my parents to be fair, but my sisters quite often saw things as negative that appeared obvious to me. Since we were used to living quite simply, my first income was easily slotted for repayment. Terry and I decided to purchase small items such as appliances, and coffee and end tables, for my parents as repayment of my loan. My sisters got upset about me doing this. They may have felt that we were bribing our parents for extra attention and they were being made to look as uncaring and unappreciative. The repayment process continued despite my sister's protests. The final payment was a Coach Tour to Nashville and Branson. My father loved Country and Western music. He had listened to the Grand Ole Opry all the years that we were growing up and living on the farm. My mom loved this music as well. It was the perfect gift and my financial commitment was paid in full.

When they returned from the trip, we were all at our house for an evening meal. While we were visiting, I spent some personal time chatting with my new brother-in-law, Ken. He was a very neat person, and was well liked by our family. Ken was quite attractive with dark, curly hair. He was average height and physically fit. After all, he worked in a Potash mine as an electrician. Ken had been employed by the Corey Potash mine for most of his life. He was President of the Steelworker's union branch, and quite over-cautious about safety. While we were having a strong discussion about unions, I got the strange feeling that Ken would never, ever visit our house again. I needed to value this discussion because there would not be many more in the future. I studied him as we talked, but didn't dwell on my feelings, just let them go.

Ken must have been feeling that something wasn't right either because around that time he arranged with the Catholic priest to be baptized. Nobody knew any reason for it; he just wanted to receive this sacrament. There was no RCIA commitment during that time in the church so his request was immediately granted. My sister, Geri, had all her children baptized because she insisted that it was very important to her. She never gave reasons but just acted on her desire. They didn't attend church, but for whatever reason, all her family had to be baptized. Geri was strange that way because she had such a strong personality; people liked her and always wanted to be around her. She made friends easily, and sometimes I have to admit being jealous of all the attention she received from everybody. Geri was very beautiful and knew how to always appear at her best. She bought elegant clothes and looked amazing in them. She had a tall, slender look that was admirable. Geri always bought various items, and if people admired them, she would give them to the person. She always shared with me and I loved her more than ever. Geri had a kind of unconditional love for all people and it was always difficult to leave her. She was friendly and kind, with a personality to be admired. You read earlier how I always admired my sister as I was growing up, and even though the years passed, that didn't change. It was neat that she would always be my sister and I would never have to fear losing time with her. She was truly special. I just wished that she could quit smoking. Geri had health problems because of her smoking, but never accepted that cigarettes were the fault. She would try all types of therapies and medications, but never could manage to quit smoking.

One day, while I was teaching at school, my life changed in a big way. It is that phone call that you never wish to receive. During the afternoon recess in early May, the vice-principal came to fetch me from the library. He walked me to his office and told me that the telephone call was for me. When I picked up the receiver, Terry was on the line. That is when he told me, Ken had been killed at the Corey Potash mine earlier in the day. I found this news difficult to believe. Don't these things only happen to other families? The office staff knew that something tragic had happened and one of the instructional assistants offered to drive me home immediately. We could get my car another time. I was in no condition to drive myself. The world wasn't real and this wasn't happening to me.

My parents and sister let us know that they were leaving for Saskatoon right away. Terry and I couldn't afford the expense of meals and a motel room so we debated about what to do next. I only knew that I desperately wanted to be with Geri. I was moving in a fog as the afternoon melted into evening. Packing would need doing anyway, so I started putting some clothes into a suitcase. The children came home from school and needed to hear the horrible news as well. What had really happened? The breaking news was now splashed all over the television channels. It was announced that Ken Wiebe had been electrocuted and died in hospital a short time later while working at the Corey Potash mine earlier in the day. What it didn't say and we learned later in Saskatoon was how Ken was upset that the government was trying to privatize the mine by cutting back on safety standards and staff. They wanted to justify the sale and make it look like the mine was losing profit. Where two electricians worked to back up each other, only one was scheduled for that day.

Ken had decided to work only half the shift on that particular day and make up time later on. It was the day before my sister's birthday and he wanted to surprise her with lunch, a card, present, and flowers. She had employment as well and arranged for the afternoon, with great anticipation. Ken had finished his shift when the power for the big mining machine started cutting in and out. He went back and did the necessary repair, but it only would work for a little while. Ken was on his way to the mine lift, when he got called back once again. He opened the power box again to try something different. The electrical staff on duty during the earlier shift had made some adjustments to the wiring system but failed to instantly update the manual. Ken had followed procedure but it was incorrect. When he attached some wires and turned the power back on, he was immediately electrocuted underground. The men described it as one of the most horrible memories they would ever have to deal with. Ken was rushed above ground, while CPR was attempted, but pretty much died instantly. He was rushed to hospital for possible revival. Nothing worked. He was dead. Geri was called to the hospital but it was already too late. That is when we got the terrible news.

After the packing was completed, I was still very restless. I needed to do something because my mind was working overtime. While I was taking a quick bath, something inside told me to drop everything, stop worrying about small problems, and get to Saskatoon as soon as possible. Reality was telling me that we couldn't afford to be gone for several days, but my heart was saying go at once. Your sister needs you. I gave in and decided to follow my heart. Quickly, I asked Terry if it was possible for us to make plans and leave that minute. He agreed and admitted that he was thinking the same thoughts. We made a few phone calls and left for Saskatoon.

Upon arriving in Saskatoon, we checked into a motel, dropped off our suitcases and sadly moved on to my sister's house. With big hugs and tears, we found a very somber group of people waiting for us. Geri was glad that I was there for her and said so. I now felt that coming to Saskatoon was the right thing to do even if we had some debt to pay off. Co-workers of Kens, neighbours and family would constantly come and go for the next several hours, offering their condolences and support. It seemed so strange that I was at his home, but Ken would not be returning that night, or ever. The feeling of something huge missing was very strong in the house. People were crying, telling stories, and generally comforting each other. Since my sister was employed by a funeral home, there already was a plot for her and her husband. The arrangements would be handled by them as well, so there wasn't much to do in preparation. Participants in the funeral ceremony were from the union and the mine, plus some government officials. Ironically, Ken was devoted to ensuring high safety standards for the mine and had many awards for his efforts. It was hard to see that with all his extra caution, he should die in such a fashion. I often wondered if Ken had some preexisting notion that something like this would happen. Of course, working in a mine is a dangerous job, but many people do it for a lifetime without having such a horrific accident.

After the funeral service was complete, family members returned to my sister's house. She had many people crowded around her and they were conversing. At that time, I felt my gaze pulled in her direction. The voice inside my heart was warning me that I would only have my sister for the following two years and then no longer. I pulled away and glanced in a different direction. The strong feeling was not to be ignored. It said that I can pretend not to hear and miss out on valuable time. My choice should be to make wise use of that time so that I can carry her memory into my future. By this point in my life, I knew that something this strong needs to be heeded, even if I am incorrect. Plus, what would I lose by making the time ahead very valuable? I could only gain from it. When we went to settle payment at the motel, we were informed that it was paid for by the Corey Potash Mine management. We didn't have to worry about any costs, they were covered.

Knowing that the time ahead with my sister would be limited, I arranged more visits with her and she constantly encouraged them. I made bus trips to Saskatoon for the weekend and she came to spend weekends with us. We enjoyed shopping and tried to spend time with our youngest sister, who lived in Saskatoon as well. One time, we strangely bought the same birthday card for dad. Geri sent hers from Saskatoon and I gave dad mine in Regina. As a teacher, I arranged for her to do presentations about the mining industry in Saskatchewan for the grade seven and eight students. Geri put together information and a video. The students loved her and she did great. Of course, we always arranged to go for lunch that day.

Eventually, she met some new gentlemen, and they were serious about her. Geri didn't really show much interest in them. She no longer appeared content and I felt that she was merely passing time. Geri gave me strong feelings of searching for something. Nothing was filling the huge void in her life and she was struggling with each day. She had told me about the pain of losing Ken and that horrible first night after it happened. Geri had waited for everyone to leave the house. She got in her car and drove to the outskirts of Saskatoon. There she sat on a secluded hill and wept alone until morning. She knew that she had to return and face the day. People would be looking for her and there were many things that needed doing. I could only imagine how much pain she was suffering. I tried not to cry in front of her because she wouldn't want me to.

About two years later, on Valentine's Day, mom and dad invited the family to their house for supper. Geri was visiting in Regina. She had sold the house in Saskatoon soon after Ken's death. My sister moved to Invermere, British Columbia and later to Cold Lake, Alberta, where she was residing at that time. She had somewhat returned to being the person that I remembered her to be, but was still very restless. Geri had called the family to update us on her latest news. I was pondering that maybe she met some fellow and was serious about him. The news was not positive though. It was a shock. Geri told us that she had been diagnosed with pancreatic cancer and had probably a couple of months to live. She was planning on moving back to Regina for her final days and wished to be buried beside Ken in Saskatoon. Geri was planning to refuse hospital admittance and treatment as much as possible. It was too late for either chemotherapy or radiation. She was not going to allow any treatment and wanted to live out her final days in a small apartment with someone to care for her. Geri would hire a caregiver to deal with her illness.

We were shocked beyond words. Yet, we knew that our sister was persistent when she set her mind to something. Geri sold most of her personal belongings or gave them to people of choice. Then, she rented an apartment in south Regina and settled in. She only allowed us to visit her the first while after she moved and still looked fairly healthy. As the sickness progressed, Geri refused any visits, except for her children and caregiver. There was a short time that she was admitted into the hospital for treatment. I went to visit her with an armful of red roses. The afternoon went much too quickly and I had to leave. Once again, I had to tear myself away without crying. If I started crying at that time, I would have probably never stopped, so the tough inside core said that luxury was not allowed. The stay was brief and she returned to her apartment, under doctor supervision. Geri was getting medication to manage the pain. She was not getting any other treatment.

One night after her return home from the hospital, my sister phoned me and we had a good, long talk. Geri informed me about all the pain that she was feeling. Most times, the medication didn't come near to dealing with the hurt. Days would go by and there would be no relief. What she told me was horrible beyond words and I felt helpless.

I wanted to help her but there was nothing that I could do but listen and love her. She was strong and she wanted me to be strong, but the agony was great. She told me about the struggle to eat and that most food didn't stay down. Geri was living a nightmare with her illness. Rare phone calls and information were updating us as to her decline. My parents, sister and I were trying our best to communicate about what we were learning and passing it on to each other. No visits were allowed. When the cancer was progressing into its final stages, Geri phoned mom and dad to allow them a final visit. She never did allow other visits for anybody, except me.

Geri phoned me one night. It had been almost two months since her announcement and I knew that the end was near. It was during the week and I was preparing for teaching the next day. Since it was Wednesday night, she asked if I would stop by her apartment after work the following day, which would be Thursday. My fear was great, knowing that she would now look thin and frail. I hadn't seen her since the hospital visit. She had looked very thin at that time already. I wanted to see her in the worst way, and yet didn't want to see her either. I drove to her apartment after work.

As I had suspected, she was mostly a shell of her former self. Her skeleton could be seen through the thin, transparent skin covering it. She was wearing some neat, patterned, flannel pajamas. Her hair was short but neatly combed and she was wearing some makeup. We immediately embraced and held each other, but I was afraid that she would break at my touch. She directed me to the sofa beside her chair. Geri sat down in a large armchair mostly covered with cushions. I was pleased that she was still able to walk alone, but only for a couple of steps. My sister looked directly at me and said, "I want you to write my obituary for the newspaper." Shock doesn't express what I felt at that moment. It was the furthest thing that I expected to hear. "No tears allowed," kept playing through my mind at that point, "the last thing that she needs is a crybaby. So, focus on the task at hand and think of nothing else."

We proceeded with the preliminary information, while enjoying a cup of tea. Geri and I browsed over examples from the newspaper and discussed how we could replace words with our own. It seemed unreal. Maybe, we were just writing a short wedding or party invitation, but certainly not my sister's death notice. Anyway, we managed to focus on the writing for a while. I was struggling to stay positive, well aware that I didn't wish to make her upset, knowing that was why she had allowed this visit. She had a job for me to do and I would focus on doing my best work. Finally, when most of the project was finished, she began telling me about the previous night. The words she said will stay with me for my entire lifetime.

My sister told me that she had taken her strongest medication to help with the nighttime and possibly allow her to sleep. She was lying in bed and trying to get somewhat comfortable without success. The pain was so great that she couldn't bear it and the medicine wasn't helping. In fact, her dosages were becoming larger and she wasn't really concerned about an overdose at this point, but just relieving the pain. The night was going to be awful without much sleep and great discomfort. It was well past midnight and her assumptions were correct. It was another horrible night that would never end. From somewhere, Geri felt soothing warmth and arms slowly wrapping around her. She was gently lifted onto someone's lap and placed comfortably in place. The pain completely disappeared and she felt unbelievably wonderful. Geri was held and cradled, while she slept, throughout the rest of the night. She woke up in the morning and all the pain was still gone. The supernatural being, whom she called Jesus, warned her that she would have the next couple of days without pain so she should finish what needed to be done. After that time, He would come back for her and she would leave. It would be time for the final business to end. At the moment, she was experiencing little to no pain and felt unusually fine, even though most of her organs had shut down. She began to look tired and I offered to leave. Geri got up from her chair for a last hug. She said these words to me, "never be afraid that God will give you more than you can handle. The next time I see you, I will be there to greet you with a big smile and hug." We hugged again and I left. Strangely, I never really felt that we were saying good-bye, but only see you in a while.

Even during her funeral at Holy Child Roman Catholic Church, I never felt like she was really gone. I could still feel her so very near. Her son, Paul Jr., says that he can often feel her near him as well. Paul became a Pentecostal minister after my sister's death. I wished that he would have practiced his faith in the Catholic Church, since he is my godchild, but I am proud of what he has chosen anyway. We are still very close and love to spend time together. Paul is the person who I feel the most comfortable discussing my faith with. He really understands and experiences many similar things as I do relating to his mother.

After her death, Geri never did feel far away. During the next number of years, she would come and visit me in dreams. One time I woke up after seeing her seated on an arch above where I was standing in my dream. The arch was decorated in wondrous flower arrangements with intertwined green branches. She was dressed in a white robe, while looking healthy and happy. Another dream took place during most of the night. We had the most beautiful talk. Geri and I were seated at the table playing cards. I remember a table with a red and white checkered table cloth. It was a wooden rectangle and wooden kitchen chairs surrounded it. Geri and I talked about everything and anything, just like in the past. When I woke up, I realized that my sister had to leave. I know that those were dreams but I experienced her presence in love and joy. Having that time together was a gift that God had allowed. I miss her terribly. We are still really connected and I am sure that she will be there waiting for me when my time comes.

CHAPTER 9:

some events of note during my working years

It was a year after my brother-in-law, Ken's death, and my school year assignment was at one school only. I was excited that now I could finally be a complete part of a staff without sharing my time. It would be good to focus on getting to actually know the students instead of seeing them in a casual, lesson for today, kind of way. I had met many great people up to this point, but always felt that I never really belonged. A lady that I had met earlier when I was substituting was on the staff at this school. Terrie and I developed an immediate friendship and enjoyed spending personal time together as well. My assignment was to do Library classes with all the grades in the school, from Kindergarten to grade eight. I would spend an hour with each class doing a book exchange and some other activity of choice. The classroom teacher would get one hour each week for preparation work. Instantly, I got involved with the workings of the school.

The eight or more years that I spent at this school were packed with learning and activity. I eventually expanded my teaching assignment and took on subject content areas. While doing grade eight Social Studies, I organized events such as Citizenship courts and Multicultural lunches. There were Halloween haunted houses in the library, Christmas concerts at the Performing Arts Center where I supervised students from all grades and got to run the big overhead spotlight, excursions, author visits with various classes, spring talent shows, and evening dances to be chaperoned. I was extremely busy because all these events occurred while I was still teaching and looking after the library, which is a full time job all on its own. I had grade seven and eight library volunteer students both male and female, but their time had to be organized and supervised. When the Scholastic book fair happened, I had to search for parent volunteers to assist with sales. Quite often I would be teaching in the classroom while other classes were browsing or shopping at the book fair. In the spring, time was spent at the large book display set up to showcase the new materials put out by various publishing companies. The rows of tables offered all the new resources that could be purchased to complement the curriculum of the time for all grade levels. I committed most of the library budget on these new resources. At year end, I participated in the grade eight farewells at Holy Family church. My fear of public speaking began to disappear. I became comfortable working and being observed in front of people. In fact, one day I walked into the library and the Director of our school system was sitting at a table and remained to watch me teach the class. There was no time to be nervous that day.

Sadly during the year, some grade eight girls made allegations about misconduct from a teacher on staff. Most of us who knew the person well didn't believe that they had misbehaved after school hours upon returning from a sports event. Unfortunately and sadly, the teacher attempted self harm, feeling that there was no other recourse. The tone of that year became subdued since staff began feeling threatened. I feared as well since a couple of the grade eight boys would come in the library after school hours, hide out, and often frighten me. On an April fool's day, while I was having my lunch and correcting assignments, they snuck in the library. The boys wound a large rope around the doorknob and circulation desk. They secured the rope so that I could not exit from the small room behind the library book shelves, and thus I was unable to leave. Being afraid, when I realized that I was imprisoned, I began to pound on the door. After much laughter and delight with their trick, the boys did undo the rope and freed me.

God was discreetly present during those years, but I didn't always recognize his great gifts until the surprise caught my attention. There were events that were quite unusual. For example, at the close of one school day in late spring, three ladies were visiting in a small nurse's room beside the front door. The window was slightly open and rain was coming down. Being absorbed in their conversation, the women didn't pay attention to what was happening. A bolt of lightning streaked between where they were standing straight to the electrical outlet in the wall. It moved in a straight line but they were positioned in a way that it did not hit any of them. What a beautiful, strange miracle that nobody was hurt. One of those ladies was married to a sports announcer for CTV news. I got to know her and became casual friends. When she learned that I had invited the special needs students that I had taught previously to a floor hockey game, she arranged to have the news cameras come to the school and interview us. It was very special to be interviewed from the school and talk about how the students were being taught to respect all people. A segment from the floor hockey game, in which the regular grade eight students were handicapped by tying scarves and using braces to limit their movement or putting them in wheelchairs, etc. was shown as well.

Throughout all the years of our marriage, Terry's musical talent with drumming have factored in. At first, he was playing in his dad's old time band, as mentioned earlier. Over time, after his father's heart attack, Terry started searching for other musical groups and became known in the old time music circles. Terry would comment that he loved old time music but wished that he would get the opportunity to do something different. Since dances occur mostly at night and on the weekends, it made our religious commitments very difficult. It seemed that I was visiting more bars and nightclubs than churches. During all those years, I would ask God how Terry's music and talent could ever factor into our faith. I would be praying and pondering if this would ever become any kind of possibility. Drums were not even a consideration at church in that time period. They would not be allowed. Even guitars were still being introduced but they were thought to be more acceptable.

Terry was working at the university of Regina library when a fellow staff member inquired about his drumming skills. The lady attended Holy Cross church and her husband was part of the music ministry. The group was interested in adding a drummer but hesitated with concern about the noise level. Terry came to a practice and the group decided to give the drums a try at the next Mass. When Terry arrived at the church, with his drums already set up, he discovered a barricade around the set. He was slightly nervous with the idea that he was one of the first musicians to play drums at church during a Mass. What if the congregation is offended? What if he is too loud or makes a mistake? Terry's concern was unnecessary because he was quiet and controlled enough that they removed the dividing screen for the next Mass and asked him to continue. He was a hit with the group and the drums were there to stay. Now many Regina churches have a drum kit and use the drums with their music ministry. My prayers were answered after all those years. At present, we often attend Mass several times on a weekend when one of Terry's two music groups is scheduled. He gets offers to play at other churches, even would get paid for doing so, but is busy enough with what he is already doing. Through his connection with people in the church, Terry began playing for musical play productions and more popular music groups. The church connection would lead Terry in his quest to play with very talented musicians.

One day, my parents received an invitation to my cousin's wedding in Melville. My mother was refusing to drive with my father on many occasions because he was experiencing difficulties that frightened her. Dad wouldn't recognize the distance of the car to the yellow highway dividing lines for two-way traffic. Sometimes he would be driving partly in the lane of opposing traffic and sometimes on the median close to the ditch. Mom and dad wished to attend the wedding and Terry generally drove them to locations upon their request. In fact, they counted on him to a great extent. A problem arose because Terry had a dance he was committed to for that particular weekend. They asked me to drive them to Melville. I still fear highway driving to this day, though I can be persuaded when necessary. Sharla and I decided we would drive my parents to the wedding. For all the weeks prior to the wedding, I prayed every night that I wouldn't encounter semi-trucks on the highway, but felt that the request was futile. The highway to Melville is one of the busier ones. I would be driving on the same highway that my accident had occurred years earlier, without Terry's support. When the weekend arrived, I built up my confidence and knew that I could succeed. With all the praying, I was hoping that God would help me with my challenge. Surprisingly, upon returning back to Regina on the Sunday afternoon and delivering my parents safely to their home, I realized that once again my prayers were completely answered. I hadn't seen one semi-trailer truck that whole weekend while driving both ways, to and from Melville. God really does spoil me!

A number of years later, a new superintendent took over the assignment for the school that I was teaching at. Since I never had a group of students to call my own, I filled a transfer form requesting a possible classroom assignment. That was a huge mistake. As the school year was ending; the principal came into the library to inform me that I was being put at two schools again. At one school, I would be doing 40% of my assignment which would include Teacher Preparation time and the Learning Resource Program. The remaining 60% at another school would be doing the Library program which included Teacher Preparation time and the Extended Learning program. I couldn't believe that they were asking one person to be pulled in so many directions. Many of these areas are specialized and teachers are asked to attend meetings and professional development. I couldn't possibly do all of it. Plus, I would be traveling every day of the week, except one, between the two schools. After getting this news, the following morning, I couldn't get out of bed with the worst back pain that I ever had in my life. Terry had to tie my shoes because I couldn't. Knowing that this was stress related, I had to deal with the situation. I decided to let some of my professional life decrease and increase personal time. A daily exercise routine was my answer. It was a good choice because I starting feeling better and love exercising to this day.

When that school year started, I encountered the most awesome staff members that I would ever meet. It seemed that once again God came to my aid. Since we only had one vehicle and Terry couldn't get me from the university each lunch hour, one lady gave me a ride when I couldn't walk between the two schools. The office managers and teachers were supportive beyond belief. Even though that was my toughest assignment, it ended up being one of my favourite years because of the wonderful people I was working with. The following year, that same superintendent was going to have me do the same thing again, but I had to stand firm and refuse. I visited our family doctor and explained what was happening. He wrote a letter to the school board office advising them of the health risks. If I was to encounter any health issues due to their staffing, they would be liable and I would be granted medical leave immediately. I got a phone call and went for a meeting at central office. My assignment was changed to one school only after that. I would be now teaching only Library, teacher preparation and the Extended Learning program. This assignment was one of my favourite.

Everything was wonderful because I was back at one school again and getting to know all the students. My classes to teach were mainly with Social Studies, Science and Health, plus the Library skills and book exchange. There was a grade six class that I really enjoyed. On a particular day, the final one before the Christmas holiday, a girl in the class was really excited. She stopped me from leaving the classroom to tell me her plans. She looked at me with the most beautiful, smiling face to relate how she and her family had made reservations to go skiing in Alberta. She mentioned how her mother was terribly frightened when forced to drive a particular stretch of the number one highway by Gull Lake. Her mom was relieved because her aunt's boyfriend was traveling with them and had offered to take this responsibility from her. We chatted on for some time and I wished her a wonderful vacation. Once again a strange feeling told me that this conversation was leading to something unfortunate. I ignored the feeling that I would never see her again and it quickly vanished. I continued to see the look of her face as the day moved on and proceeded into the holiday break. In fact, I can still see the timeless look all these years later. A few days before the return from holidays, we learned that she and her mom had been killed in a head-on collision. It was on that particular stretch of highway that they feared and the boyfriend was driving. The school students grieved for her long afterwards and I did as well.

There is humour in some accounts of when I have encountered God's intervention. Some may even say that He had nothing to do with this, but since I lived it, I feel differently. The Resource Center of a school where I was teaching was located in the middle of the school and shared a wall with the Multi-Purpose room. It was very small, cramped and dark inside. There was no work space for the teacher-librarian. The library door connects to a small room, used by a nurse or dental technician in the past. When I began teaching full time at the school, I asked the administrator if I could use the small space for my teaching assignment, since I had no place for my personal teaching materials. He immediately told me that the room was not available to me at all. I would have to store my resources on the top of a small filing cabinet and the door would be blocked by shelves on the other side. The small room was now intended for use as storage for Guided reading leveled resources. Because the library shelving was already overused, I felt that some French kits, approximately twenty some of them, could be stored on the top shelf in the little room. They looked terrible on the library top shelf because the ceiling dropped in that area and it was extremely dark. I moved all those kits into the small room one day after school. A grade one teacher complained to our administrator and the following day he came and requested that I move them back into the library.

Feeling very angry and put out about the unfairness of what had just happened, I went to work and returned them to the library. The space in the little room wasn't needed and it felt like favouritism to me.

The following morning when I returned to school, I noticed some water marks in the ceiling that were never there before. When I glanced at the ceiling, I noticed that a substantial water leak was right over the top shelf that housed the French kits. I immediately took a stool and dragged the kits all down on to the floor. They would be ruined if they stayed up on the shelf. Calling in our administrator, I showed him the water still trickling down from the ceiling. He called out the necessary personnel to make the repair. It took them a couple of days, but they found the leak. They replaced the ceiling tiles and assured us that everything was back in good repair. So, I had no choice but to return the French kits back on the top shelf. Strangely, the next morning when I returned to the school, water was once again trickling down in the newly repaired space. I contacted our administrator and he had me set the kits on the floor. Once again, the system plumbers and repair team tore apart the ceiling area and remedied the problem. It may be difficult to believe, but this time I thought that the replaced kits would be on the top shelf once and for all. It was not meant to be. For the third time, we went through the whole repair process. I would laugh hysterically when alone in the room because some strange phenomena allowed me to get rid of the detested French kits and reclaim my library space. The administrator eventually relented and allowed the kits to stay in the little room. I said, "Thank you God for my small victory." When I visited the school a few years after completing my assignment there and I had transferred to another school, the first thing I noticed was the return of the French kits to the top library shelf. I didn't care this time because it wasn't my working space any longer.

While I had still been attending university and taking my last class, I unexpectedly met someone who was hired to teach at Notre Dame College in Wilcox, Sask. I had mentioned this strange encounter in one of my previous chapters. Because we had spent a month working and learning together, we developed a comfortable friendship. For some unexplained reason, I decided to arrange for the Notre Dame choral to perform at the school that I was teaching at. The performance was a tremendous success with the entire school student body. The intent of the arranged visits was to teach how music could be an option in high school. The musical talent and choreography were top rate. I hoped that it would encourage more musical participation for the young students. The production was always a success and the Notre Dame students were treated as 'Stars'. A few years later when I was transferred to another school, I invited the choral to perform there. The choral was successful there as well. Terry was continuously sought to supply music with the choral throughout many years to come due to the new contact. He was asked to travel with the choral to many out of town locations. Terry boasts six decades as part of the music section of the Notre Dame choral, whenever his talent was needed. Making the arrangements for the concerts was time consuming, but definitely worth the effort.

CHAPTER 10:

my adult family and a new parish

Life was once again flowing peacefully. We became a part of our new neighbourhood. The beginning was very rocky and unstable. We felt many times that we had made another mistake by moving to our condominium as mentioned earlier. The neighbours continuously never hesitated to inform us that we weren't wanted here with children and would never be welcome or fit in. They did not want any children around them at all. We constantly assured them that our son and daughter would not cause any problems. It made no difference. Many complaints were continuously lodged against us. Sharla was a nuisance because she wanted to roller skate in front of our garage after school and she could ruin the concrete. Shane had a portable basketball hoop and stand that could be assembled and taken apart when he was finished playing. Complaints were sent to us that he bounced the ball and it agitated the neighbours. They wanted him to carry the sports equipment out to the main street to be used. My children got shunned because they eventually bought vehicles and needed to park in front of our house. We couldn't do anything right. No matter how much permission we asked for we were never successful. Sometimes we would receive written warnings from the condominium board placed where we would find them.

After arriving home from school one day, the phone rang. Our next door neighbour was on the other end. He informed me that Terry had shovelled off the deck and deliberately thrown snow against his house. Our condominium units are very close and only an asphalt walkway provides space. Terry tried to keep the snow on our own side of the pathway but there was too much of it. I couldn't believe the amount of minor and pathetic stories lodged against us. Terry contemplated becoming a board member until the surrounding members formed a circle and decided to veto him. They were looking for new members but I guess that didn't include us. What do you do when you don't feel welcome in your neighbourhood? I just ignored as much as I could because we were gone most of the time anyway. Eventually, we closed our doors and windows in secluded privacy. I really felt badly for my children because they were dealing with bullying at school and being rejected when we got home. We had to stay. This was our home now and there was no way that we could afford to move. Plus, I loved our condo unit and didn't want to move. It was beautiful and developed throughout as we wanted it to look.

Shane and Sharla persevered because they had family support and love. They knew that their parents loved them and would do anything within their capability to make them happy. With our family unit strong, we could deal with the rest. When Shane and Sharla advanced into high school, they both progressed and were happy. Shane became involved in sports and made many new friends. Sharla joined students that were artistically creative and her reading skills were an asset. She was invited into some advanced classes and got university credits for them. Sharla made new friendships that would continue into her adult life. Both my son and daughter went on to university and eventually graduated with degrees. Shane got a Bachelor of Business Administration degree and an accounting certificate from SIAST. Sharla got a Bachelor of Arts degree in English. I was thrilled that she was taking several Religious studies classes. She achieved a minor in Religious Studies. Later, she got a Master's degree after her wedding and move to Ontario, but I wish to elaborate on this time as the chapter ends.

Shane and Sharla lived at home while attending the University of Regina. One evening, I dreamed of the strongest romance that a young couple could have. It was like when you fall in love for the first time and think of nothing else. When I awoke the following morning it felt very strange to think this way. My marriage was successful and Terry and I were truly in love, but this dream was much stronger than anything I had remembered in a long time. Something unusual was going to happen and I could feel it.

The dream occurred on Halloween morning. That night Sharla was going to a university party at the Owl with some of her friends. That was the night that she met Conlan, her future husband. It seemed they were interested in each other almost immediately. How strange that the dream was a predictor of my daughter's marriage. The details are her story to tell and not mine.

While I am gaining my future son-in-law, I am losing my mother. Sadly, my mother got diagnosed with lymphoma, which is a form of cancer, early in the spring of 2002. She had concerns over a large, brown growth on her cheek by her ear, but the doctor did not validate and analyze her fears seriously. Eventually my mother insisted on having the growth examined more carefully. When the results finally came back, it was too late for cancer surgery. There was no chance of catching the cancer in the early stages any longer. Mom was very angry with her doctor because there were too many visits at his office when he didn't do anything but assure her that everything was all right and normal. She transferred to the doctor that my father was visiting. Mom really liked Dr. Cameron and he wanted to try chemotherapy even though the chances of recovery were slim. Most importantly, the doctor made my mother feel that he really cared about her.

My mother began her cancer treatments soon after being diagnosed and switching doctors. My sister Sharryl would stay with her at the hospital during her treatment and I would drive them both home afterwards while coming home from school. Even though this time was scary and uncertain, I knew that I needed to make the most of it because I had the strange feeling that mom wouldn't recover. I kept remembering all the times we went either Wednesday or Friday night shopping. Mom and dad would spend an evening with us at Wal-Mart in the Southland Mall. I could buy just about anything that was needed and mom would pay for it. Often we would go to other stores if the children needed school clothes or new clothing items for a special occasion. Mom never judged our purchases and encouraged us to have a fun evening no matter what the cost. She would always joke about just getting her pension cheques. When mom got the news and date of her first cancer treatment, we went for a final shopping trip. I knew that we would never get to shop again. I can still see her walking through every aisle more for exercise than actually shopping. She would wander so slowly that sometimes we were barely moving. The shopping cart was always in the lead, with mom pushing it and me a few steps behind her. One evening, I laugh to remember when I was so tired from teaching all day that I relaxed to the point of dozing with sleep even though we were still walking. When mom turned back to speak some comment, it made me realize that I was actually snoozing. I don't think she noticed. She may have but did not mention anything about it. During the years of my children's youth, we would all walk around the mall. Shane and Sharla would be along for the evening. When they got older, they didn't do the shopping part, but would join us for coffee at Smitty's. We always frequented the same places. Dad was responsible for the lunch payment. My parents never grew tired of their family evenings at the mall with their children and grandchildren.

Having mom's health failing was a painful time. As I watched her trying to bravely move on with her remaining days, memories that had unbelievable meaning kept surfacing. They included all the holidays that she provided for us. Mom would encourage us to travel. Terry would be the driver and our family vehicle would be used, but my mom and dad would fund the trip. We sometimes camped and other times we would stay in a motel. Places visited included Ontario, South Dakota and North Dakota. This kindness from my parents always gave us something to look forward to during the summer months.

Now I had to deal with all of these memories and beautiful events drawing to a close. Even though I knew that I was losing my mother, I didn't want to think about it. Maybe if I didn't make it feel like a reality, it wouldn't come true. My sister Sharryl and I tried to assist in any way possible. We could never come close to repay all the love and caring that our parents had provided to help raise all their grandchildren. We knew that when mom's final treatments were complete, she only showed a slight improvement. The hospital reported that she was now in remission. The passing of time would tell us for sure what the results would be.

At Christmas time, I offered to host the family at my house. Decorating for this season is one of my passions, so I was excited about having everyone from our family over. Mom and dad insisted that all costs would be covered by them and that we should order trays of food so that we wouldn't have to spend long hours of preparation. It was a joyous time but mom had to wear a head covering because of her hair loss from the cancer treatments. She was very weak and fragile, but had the determination to appear strong. Mom needed assistance moving about. It was heartbreaking to watch her trying to maneuver in the cold and snow. We did have a good Christmas in spite of all the obstacles. Even though mom was still living in her own house, my sister and I would stop there to help with household chores. Dad did many things to assist with mom's stay at home. Towards the end of January, we noticed that mom was spending her full days in bed. Early in February, we had to call the ambulance to take her for hospital care. As I watched her being carried out on the stretcher, my mind registered that she was leaving her home for the final time and would never return again. I wondered what she was thinking and how horrible that would feel. Yet, mom made it appear that she was only leaving for a while and that everything would be O.K. She wanted to always look like a strong person, without showing her true feelings.

Mom was admitted to the hospital, where we were encouraged to remain by her side. The staff was wonderful and provided to make us as comfortable as possible. While mom was still alert, we arranged for her to receive the sacrament of the sick. She responded in a full Christian way. We left the room and mom received the sacrament of Reconciliation. We all received the Eucharist and blessing as a family. We had a couple more days' together, coming and going but were constantly informed that the end was drawing near. Soon we were advised to stay at the hospital and camp out, if we wished to be with mom when she passed away. My father, sister Sharryl, Terry and I stayed with her until the very end. Some of her final words were, "I am going home now." She always had amazing faith and it was most evident at the end. It helped to hear her and see how content she was. My mother, Anne Kathleen Hanowski, passed away on February 18, 2003 at the age of 78 years. Her funeral Mass was at Holy Child church with Rev. John Weekend presiding.

Time passed and Sharla and Conlan decided to become engaged. We were overjoyed at the thought of an upcoming wedding. We really liked her choice because he was so ambitious and enthusiastic. Conlan was working tirelessly to complete two degrees, a Bachelor of Arts degree and a Bachelor of Education degree. He would spend hours on an overnight shift at the Co-Op store and then go to classes the following day at the University. Many times I wondered how he could achieve such high grades while most certainly feeling tired. Yet, he mastered all requirements and soon graduated. Sharla graduated with him at the same time. She tried obtaining work after finishing her Arts degree, but soon realized that this degree didn't offer much more than manual, sales labour. Sharla wanted to be more successful than that, so we encouraged her to apply for a Master's program. She was accepted immediately into the Master's of Library and Information Science program at the University of Western Ontario and decided to start there in the Fall Semester. Sharla was initially planning to move on to university and maybe stay in a campus dormitory. Her new boyfriend had other ideas and asked her to get married before school started. They planned a wedding date of July 17th.

It was sad and unfortunate that my mother was no longer alive to attend the wedding, but it was a beautiful affair. Terry and I have many musically talented friends. We invited them to sing at the Mass and attend the wedding. The awesome music was provided by 'Joyful Noise' at Holy Cross Church. Fr. Brian Meredith performed the wedding ceremony. Terry and I, with our family attended church regularly at Resurrection, so they had a wedding Mass. Resurrection Parish Masses had moved out of the St. Gabriel School gymnasium and were now being held in the newly constructed building. It was not ideal for holding wedding services yet, so Father recommended using another church. Conlan was not baptized at this time, but promised to become Catholic after the wedding.

Resurrection Parish was becoming a reality during the years that my children were growing up to be adults. At first, an opening Mass was held in the St. Gabriel gymnasium and I remember Fr. Norm Marcotte and Deacon Joe Lang playing a huge part in this beautiful celebration. Immediately, I decided that because I never had the opportunity to be involved at Holy Cross Church due to employment and family commitments, I would like to become a meaningful part of Resurrection. Terry still played with musical bands most weekends and I often attended church alone on Saturday evening whereas, Terry attended what was available to his schedule. If the church was close to where I lived, I could accommodate being scheduled and committed. I was afraid to offer my name at first but decided to put it on the schedule list anyway. Resurrection was recruiting for the many ministries. I could learn and update even though I hadn't been involved in a parish since Children's Liturgy many years earlier.

Yes, I had done some Mass duties when asked to do them for the school children. I was asked to distribute ashes on Ash Wednesday while at one school. I planned, implemented, and did readings for many faith liturgies over the years. It was mandatory for staff to be involved in these scheduled events. All my religious involvement, except for children's liturgy, had been for school children and mainly held in a gymnasium. Even though our Parish events were still held in a gymnasium, it was moving towards being an actual church facility and I wanted to be a part of it. First, I decided to start by being a Eucharistic minister. I would be surrounded by others who could help if I made any errors. When my name came up on the schedule, I was both very nervous and excited. In my mind, I reviewed the procedures that I had been taught during the training session. This was my first time as a Eucharistic minister. What I didn't know was that I was scheduled to do cup ministry and there was to be no cup that night. Deacon Joe was doing the Mass and the host was consecrated previously but there is no wine when that occurs. I was not sure what to do and found a seat close to the front. Just as I was about to move forward, a man from the parish blocks me with the words, "anybody knows that when there isn't a priest present that there is no cup offered. Go sit back down." Needless to say my feelings were hurt. It was not the most pleasant beginning and I felt that something explained using those words was very rude. I was not to be stopped just because of one person, so I decided that I would put the incident out of my mind and forget about it. There had to be a nicer way to encourage people to participate at a Mass. Oh well!! Fortunately, I have this stubborn streak and decided that I would perfect the skill and he would never have an opportunity to embarrass me again.

The next time that my name came on the list was an opposite experience. Two amazingly beautiful ladies were in the Vestry. Arlene and Carrie were helpful, kind and informative. Upon meeting them, I knew that I really did wish to stay and continue with being a part of the ministry at church. I could feel a strong sense of love and caring, plus being welcomed. It is what helping at a church should feel like. After all, we are in God's house. A couple of years later, I decided to add Proclaimer to my ministry list, feeling that I could be a good and powerful reader one day. The girl that was terrified of speaking in front of her friends and classmates had put her name on the list to read in front of a whole congregation. It is amazing how the Holy Spirit can make a person grow and change with an unquenchable desire to do God's will. After many years of service, I chuckle when people comment about the success of my ministries. They often state that they could never participate at Mass and appear so knowledgeable and relaxed as they see me doing. I receive many compliments, but they are not for me. God gives me the strength to do what I could never do otherwise.

CHAPTER 11:

God sends special help for a year

Sharla and Conlan's beautiful wedding day was now recent history. We prepared to move them to London, Ontario. When they returned from a short honeymoon, the newlyweds stayed at our house for a couple of weeks, at Sharla's request. She felt more comfortable still being with her family and I enjoyed having them with us. Sharla began to pack all her belongings from her bedroom. The wedding presents were now opened and being stored in our basement. I had heard of a teacher-librarian position that opened closer to our home due to a retirement. When I put in the transfer, I was accepted. All of my school teaching resources had to be boxed and relocated to our basement. The basement had the appearance of belonging to a hoarder, if a stranger would happen to see it. During all this activity, I was pondering the new space that would be available to us with my children no longer living at home. Shane was already in his own apartment since becoming employed and completing his education. The entire condominium required a renovation because all our income had previously been spent on the children's needs of education, living accommodations, and a wedding. Plus, we were funding Sharla and Conlan's move to London, Ontario, which was not going to be a cheap venture either.

If or when we eventually could get some money put aside, Terry and I would have to decide whether we wanted to begin renovations upstairs or downstairs. The whole house needed a new look because it was definitely dated and our furniture was not in the best repair either. I still had some years of teaching ahead and we thought we could concentrate on upgrading our house in the near future.

When Sharla and Conlan's big moving day for departure to Ontario arrived, the hired semi-truck was late. It was scheduled for early afternoon but only pulled in front of our house late in the day. Terry and I had some of the young couple's belongings in our van, which we would drive. The newlyweds had purchased a used car for themselves which was also loaded with items of value that they didn't wish to have placed in the moving van. Belatedly we left Regina for Winnipeg, which would be our first stop for the night. Even though the hour was late when we arrived, the travel went smoothly. Terry and I were somewhat concerned about Sharla and Conlan travelling such a long distance since neither of them was a seasoned driver. We had no choice but to continue on. It was always scary watching large semi-trucks pull up closely behind their vehicle before picking a space to pass. I felt that God was watching over us and that nothing terrible was meant to happen.

A few days later, we arrived in London, Ontario. There were times during the trip that we had to switch off driving. Everyone took turns driving the two vehicles. We made arrangements to stay in a motel for a couple of days upon arrival. The initial inspection of their suite was extremely disappointing. It was really disgusting and dirty. We had to take the landlords word as to the condition of the apartment since we rented it sight unseen over the telephone. The former tenant was very filthy and left grease and grime over everything. I was not prepared to leave my daughter and son-in-law to live in such a horrible mess. We immediately set to work washing down walls and scrubbing floors and carpets. Every room needed grease remover and minor repairs. Light bulbs were missing and baseboards were pulling apart with the mold from water damage. A great amount of time, work, and money was needed to make the place livable for them. Later in the week, Terry and I finally agreed that they would be somewhat comfortable in their new lodgings.

When the time came to leave, it was a sad farewell. It was the first time that Sharla was actually moving away from home and living in a strange city. She was a married woman with a husband, who had an education to complete. We hoped that Conlan could get some work as a substitute teacher to provide additional income to her student loan. Sharla had received some bursary money, but even with our assistance revenue would have to be added for them to survive. One of the first things they learned in Ontario was how expensive the cost of living was compared to Saskatchewan. In the beginning, it seemed that Terry and I had to continue sending them food certificates and money for insurance, loan, and rent payments. That was a very tough first year for the newlyweds, and our dream of renovations would have been once more put on hold.

God took our family matters into His own hands. I like to think of it that way because what followed was very unusual. A couple of days after arriving back home in Regina, we had a terrible storm. The severe rain came down fast and furious. Terry inspected all our property after the storm was finished. Everything seemed to be fine and undamaged. We had lived in different areas of the city, in different residences and never had any issues. The particular rainstorm that we had just experienced was different than we could have expected and it totally surprised us. All the wedding presents along with Sharla and Conlan's personal belongings were in Ontario. I was grateful to have removed all my teaching materials to the school at this point since the new school year was to begin in a few more days. The basement was quite empty, except for the older furniture that existed there.

The morning following the storm, found me still asleep from all the moving and excitement. Terry had awakened and was attempting to quietly proceed downstairs. Our computer rested on a desk in the basement and he wished to work on it to pass the time. The desk was an antique from an old train station. It had been purchased by my sister, Geri and was special to me. Terry wanted to let me continue resting. Suddenly, I could hear my name called very loudly with a, "come here quickly and see this!" At the bottom of the stairs, in his stocking feet, Terry had stepped into some smelly and slimy raw sewage. While we were sleeping overnight, the sewers had backed up and covered the floor of the entire basement from one end to the other. We immediately drove to the supermarket and bought some rubber boots. Everything that remained in the basement had to be moved upstairs before it got more soaked and damaged than it already was.

Terry phoned the insurance company and arranged for an inspection. Meanwhile, we carted boxes of Terry's record collection, items and souvenirs from trips, mementos from our children's school years, family treasures from deceased relations and much more that we were storing for our children until they could secure permanent residences. Most of the day was spent climbing up and down the stairs until all items were relocated to a spare bedroom on the main level. Some furniture such as the desk and large cabinet were too big and had to remain downstairs. We lifted whatever we could off the floor so items weren't standing immersed in the dirty water. The decision as to whether we should renovate the upstairs or downstairs had been made for us. Terry and I were getting a new basement. Compliments of Mother Nature, God, and the insurance company we would have something for ourselves to concentrate on. The storm had provided the basis for a new beginning. It was sad to have something like this happen. I felt devastated at the time, but now looked upon it as a gift. It gave us a beginning that would later lead to the whole house being redone for ourselves. We gave to our children all we could provide for their needs. Now Terry and I were being given an opportunity to have something beautiful in return. We would never have thought of such a means or considered it without divine intervention. We accidentally discovered after the storm that in the construction of the basement, some electrical wires were dangerously laying on the concrete floor. If they had ever become damaged from time and wear, we could have easily been electrocuted and not known the reason why.

I was in the home stretch of my teaching career. I was feeling very excited and experienced from all the years of teaching that I had completed. The new school staff was welcoming and hopefully, I would never be asked to move from this school until I retired. Of course, I was still doing library teaching. No matter how many requests I had made, the superintendents wouldn't consider releasing me from library duties, now I wouldn't wish to leave any longer. An older teacher-librarian close to retirement provided me with a close look at what I had and other options to consider. I was convinced that at this point in my career, a major change wouldn't be in my best interest. Besides, I started to think of the whole school as my classroom. I enjoyed working with the entire school student body at all grade levels.

When the students arrived at the first day of school, I learned that God had provided me with a beautiful, human guardian angel as well. Her name was Paula. The lady was a parent volunteer that spent every day at the school with her children while they were in their classrooms. She drove in from Balgonie but wished to stay in the city with her family. Paula was willing to help throughout the school but mostly in the library. She would do any duties that were requested of her. Paula was treated as staff. She was unsure about my reception since we hadn't met. Paula is a person that is instantly easy to like. She has a warm and humourous personality. Everything about her is amazing. We were a perfect match and became friends immediately. Paula wanted to learn anything and everything about library that I was willing to teach her. I found that she was always so easy to talk to that mostly unaware; we began confiding in each other. Even years later, after my retirement, I wish to never lose contact with her because she really knows how to be a friend and treat people with kindness and respect.

The progress and rebuilding of the basement became an icebreaker for conversation with much of the new staff. Paula and I enjoyed conversing whenever opportunity arose. She assisted with all the new things that I needed to know about the school and helped me cease-lessly to stay caught up. Library didn't mean long hours of extra work because Paula looked after everything else while I was teaching in the classroom. I also had a couple of extra parent volunteers at this school. It was great! My friend Terrie was on staff here as well. Actually, she was the reason that I decided to transfer when the previous teacher-librarian retired. Why do we sometimes get unexpected, extra help when we most need it? God provided for all my needs without me being aware of it and everything fell into a series of events that only our Creator could have perfected. I could see God's handiwork as this year progressed. Paula became my strength to lean on at work and offered the support that I so desperately needed. She seemed to understand all that I was feeling. Partly, I believe that because we were raised in a family of girls and both had older sisters, it caused us to follow a similar point of view. Paula had a unique understanding for our conversations about supernatural help and supported my belief in God.

In December of my first year, Terrie and I had gone out to lunch, as we often enjoyed doing. The weather was cool and damp with a new overnight covering of snow. Terrie and I had been friends for so many years that we were relaxingly comfortable with each other. We would forget all cares and concerns and just enjoy the moment. She knew that I disliked driving and would generally take her car. On this lunch hour, we decided to make a quick stop at Robin's doughnuts. We were laugh-ing and talking as we exited her vehicle. Not looking at the ground, I didn't realize that there was a small step up to the concrete entryway. As I stumbled, I reached out with my arm to brace from landing on my face. Terrie was concerned as I stood up. I felt alright except that my arm was throbbing. I was experiencing some numbness as well. We had limited time for lunch, so I decided that because my arm moved, it should be fine. Possibly a bruise would show up later. Upon returning to the school, there was an announcement over the intercom that all vehicles from the school parking lot should be moved to the church parking lot for snow clearance.

Attempting to open the car door sent shooting pain down my arm and a feeling of weakness. I was supposed to be in the classroom immediately after lunch, but the classroom teacher had permitted me a few minutes to move my vehicle before it was her turn. I needed to hurry. The weakness in that arm was not allowing for speed and I realized that there was something more serious than I at first anticipated. The classroom teacher was no longer present when I entered her room so I had no option but to continue with the class. Making the most of a painful situation, I persisted with my teaching until the recess break. The children were well behaved and there were no issues, only the pain was now intensifying in that arm. After recess, there was some time to work in the library so I had a reprieve but found that the pain was still present and very strong. The arm felt sore and useless. After the final bell, I couldn't see much point in staying at the school with so much discomfort. I informed the office manager about what had occurred and decided to visit the after hours medical clinic.

There was a short wait when I arrived at the medical clinic but soon the arm was examined. The doctor believed that it was fractured and sent me for an x-ray. She advised me to remain at home and rest the arm for a few days until the x-ray was confirmed. I was to arrange a visit to our family doctor in the near future. That weekend I had invited our whole family to my house. We were to celebrate dad's 89th birthday. Since mom passed away, dad had been struggling with his health. We needed to celebrate this special day with dad because we might not have many more opportunities. Actually that proved true because he soon had hospital emergency visits, and then his final stay. With my broken arm in a cloth sling, I cleaned my house, vacuumed, and prepared the house for his birthday. I was quite excited and the pain didn't feel as bad. Later, the doctor visit confirmed that the arm was fractured and I would have a cast for several weeks. The break was also on my right arm and I am right-handed. I would need a replacement teacher for a while. It was a blessing that I could prepare to hand over my assignment with Paula there to look after the library and guide the new teacher.

When I returned back to school after Christmas, the library looked great and everything worked smoothly. The replacement teacher commented on how great it was working at the school and how lucky I was to have Paula. Once again time passed and I resettled with my new assignment. Some days though, I arrived at school tired from being at the hospital until late in the night. The nursing home telephoned more often informing us that dad had been rushed to the hospital after experiencing a black out or fall. Sharryl and I were becoming more concerned all the time. We arranged to spend all the time with him that we could allow and still function with our own lives and families. Paula was a true friend and support all that time. It really helped to have someone to talk to and share my feelings with. Having her to confide in, allowed for some of the pressure and anxiety to be released.

The time came when dad was admitted into the hospital and would require a higher level of care if or when he was released. Sharryl and I went to spend time with dad every day and informed the extended family to come for visits as well. He was very uncomfortable and in pain but tried to remain positive. Each visit mirrored a decline in his health and we could feel that he was not improving. Dad probably would not be leaving the hospital this time. He was cheerful when the grandchildren, nieces and nephews visited, but fell asleep as soon as they left. Sharryl and I would sit with him quietly when we were alone and allow him to rest. He always knew when we were there and liked when we held his hand and massaged his fingers. One night we were informed dad had a very serious stroke. He was paralyzed to quite a degree. Dad was in pain and the medications were only working for a while. He didn't want anyone to touch him or to be moved at all. The medical staff didn't think that he would live much longer. Dad did struggle through one more day. During dad's final night, the doctor from Intensive care visited with Sharryl and me. She wanted to know about life support and stressed the additional pain it would add to his remaining life. We both agreed that dad would want us to let him go. There would be no life support. He would die naturally. My father, William Lenard Hanowski passed away on Sunday, June 12th, 2005 at the age of 89 years. He was buried out of Holy Child Roman Catholic Church with Father John Weckend presiding. Dad loved talking about his years in the army. He would have been proud and overjoyed when Klaus played the Last Post on his trumpet for him at the funeral. I was glad that we celebrated his final birthday in December, even though my arm was broken. I had missed a week of school because of the funeral and preceding preparations. Once again, I was blessed with Paula's assistance during my absence.

When mom passed away, it was very difficult, but when dad passed away, it meant that both of our parents were now gone. At first there were many preparations and family events to organize. The younger generation looked to us for consolation. There was much visiting and reminiscing. Like everything in life, eventually all people have to return to the regular day to day routines. I thought that it would be good to have time to myself again but found that I was terribly wrong. In fact, my life became quite unhappy. I had always been dad's girl even though he showered love on everybody. My father was the person whom I had spent most of my time with as I was growing up. He treated me as the son he never had by teaching me how to drive the tractor, allowing me to help with the harvest, giving me farm animals to own, and most of all explaining how to work on the farm and repair implements. It wasn't important that I demonstrate the knowledge, he was happy just to pass it on.

At first, I was just sad and tired. I knew that it was part of the grieving process. After a while, I would busy myself with all the duties that I could possibly fit into a day. I wanted to be exhausted so my mind would be too tired to think. Strangely, instead of moving forward with my life, I felt that I was moving backwards into more sadness and depression. I just didn't seem to be able to move into the new day. Nothing excited or interested me. Nights were the worst. When my head would hit the pillow, it seemed that my mind started working overtime. I would have trouble falling asleep. When I would wake up in the middle of the night, usually around two o'clock or so, memories would come flooding back to me. I would remember all the love for my dad and how I feared losing him, especially when I was a child. Quite often, I wouldn't fall asleep after that but just toss, turn and weep until morning. The middle of night grief was continuing for well past a year and wouldn't subside. One night I woke up about the usual time. The same sequence of feelings started again and I could feel myself tense up. I knew that I was now wide awake and feeling the pain of the memories. Suddenly, I felt like I was compelled to sit upright. Immediately I could feel the simple, commanding and straightforward words, "he's with me." Instantly, almost by magic, the pain and sadness disappeared. A new calm took its place that felt like the bright, white space experienced after my car accident. The place had a feeling of love that can't be described. It made you want to stay there forever, wrapped in endless beauty and tranquility. I fell into a soft, restful sleep immediately. When I awoke the following morning, I was completely surprised by what had just happened and couldn't comprehend it. The sun was now shining but I couldn't remember the time that had lapsed in between. I was rested and feeling quite content. After that night, I never woke up in sorrow again. I also never felt the need to be upset and grieve for him any longer. I could talk about my father and share memories without tears. I believe God told me that he had my father with him. He couldn't possibly be in any better hands.

Sharla and Conlan missed my father's funeral because they were still in Ontario. She didn't like living there and pressed to complete her Master's Degree program. The following August, Sharla had finished university and they decided to return to Regina. Conlan eventually got some teaching assignments but most of the year, we did have to support them financially. We were hoping that he could find some teaching work with the new school year starting soon. Paula stayed with me full time for the first year. The second year, she was offered a half time position at Information and Library Services. She would still come back and help me for the remaining half day, then take her children home after school. The following year she accepted full time employment. Paula still works in the library and we occasionally cross paths when I am substituting. We make an effort to spend an evening together when Terry performs at the Christ the King show.

CHAPTER 12:

unfair treatment

My son-in-law, decided to follow his dream and educational training. He wished to pursue a teaching career upon returning to Regina from London, Ontario. What happened to him should never be allowed to happen to anyone. The cruel treatment towards him was beyond belief and the impact of what happened changed our family permanently in both a positive and negative way. This is his story.

Conlan could be introduced as a very special young person. He has talents in many different areas. He has a double degree in Arts and Education. He is hard working and never lacks showing extra effort when needed to make things work. Conlan is an artist and is skilled in sculpting, painting and drawing. He is athletic, capable of coaching many sports and demonstrates great skills with working around youth. Plus, he can do wonders with technology.

Upon returning to Regina, both of the young couple needed to pursue employment. They both had an education but now needed the experience necessary to complement it. I went down to the school board main office and had Conlan apply for work as a substitute teacher since the new teacher's were already hired for the upcoming school year. He was immediately placed on the list and started being called to work. Sharla applied for several positions and was accepted at the Regina Public Library for a one year position.

It became instantly evident that our son-in-law was succeeding when he was requested repeatedly by many teachers. The first year was successful because, even though he was substituting, Conlan was working almost full time. He enjoyed the work and was really thriving. Since he was still fairly new there was no position offered to him for the second year. Conlan had registered in the Rite of Christian Initiation of Adults or RCIA, soon after substitute teaching. His registration was through the Parish where Terry and I attended. While growing up, Conlan's parents never had him baptized and believed that it should be his choice as an adult. During the drive to apply for teaching, he and I had the serious conversation about faith as a belief system and not a means to acquiring a job. He assured me that his intentions were sincere.

The RCIA program at that time was not without its problems. The instruction and content were lacking and there were often questions that didn't make sense. Whoever was doing the teaching may have been unfamiliar with what they were presenting and I could not justify to him what I would be hearing. We would have discussions and he would ask me questions that were taught but that I didn't believe as true and factual to my faith and church. He was frustrated and so was I. How could I encourage my son-in-law in what I didn't believe myself? One night he asked me to sit in a session with him. They were teaching about the role of women in the church and why they participate as they do. After an extremely sexist and infuriating discussion, I could not justify him continuing with such a limited view of matters. The next day, at school, I was sharing some of my frustration with the Office Manager. She felt that the program at Holy Child was more established and would better facilitate his needs and questions. The lady was correct because the program was completed there. Conlan really liked all the people and Fr. John Weckend baptized and confirmed him when the day arrived. It was beautiful to see my son-in-law become part of our church and faith.

The second year of substitute teaching was completed with as much enthusiasm and success as the first year. Terry and I were beginning to feel that Conlan should now be offered more permanent employment, since he had already proven himself. At this point, classroom teachers were requesting him for replacement and temporary contracts. Conlan continued into a third year of substituting. Eventually contract work took him to the end of the school year. We had high hopes that Conlan was well on his way to fulfilling what he was striving for. He needed to find success as an employed husband, since Sharla by this time was working in an out-of-scope position at SaskPower. After one year at the Regina Public Library, they decided that they didn't need new librarians at that time. Sharla was terminated but a supervisor recognized the true talent that she had. The rest is history because a position was available at SaskPower and Sharla was hired for it. She is still there and finding her work rewarding.

September returned and another new school year had begun. Terry and I were feeling positive that this year would be successful. The professional journey that Conlan was taking meant much to me since I had been mentoring and guiding him over the last few years. It was a personal battle for me as well because I had seen all his talents and demanded high standards of him. Conlan had done presentations and several guest lessons for me over the years because of all his artistic and technological talent. I knew what he was capable of if he was given the opportunity. I was frustrated over the many years he had already substituted but sometimes job growth and experience take time. He was being lead to believe that good substitute teachers were needed in our school system as well. This may be true, but I was seeing teachers with less ability than him getting hired for permanent jobs because they happened to be friends with certain administrators. I had also seen many young hopefuls on the substitute list for years on end, feeling that next year would be their turn. I was beginning to lose patience with the system but had no control and felt helpless.

A telephone call came requesting a temporary replacement contract for Conlan to accept one morning while he was substituting at my school of employment. He was excited and delighted. Our Office Manager mentioned an offside alert to me that was quite unusual. She commented, "Pat, be cautious with this assignment. When the administrator called in the request, she was negative about it. She said that she didn't know Conlan and wasn't aware of him in our system. He couldn't be a good teacher if he wasn't an acquaintance of somebody that she already knew." Those words were really scary for an administrator to use. How do you really prepare someone who is terribly excited and motivated? Conlan was on his own this time and I couldn't really help nor guide him.

The contract was for about three months, ending around Christmas time. The administrator proved true to her word and only she knows why she was not willing to show compassion to a young teacher. She was not willing to show kindness or assist him in any way. Some boys in a grade six classroom did not feel that they should be assigned homework to assist in their learning process. They felt because their teacher was only a substitute that he didn't need to be obeyed. The parents were ill informed and met with the school administrator. She totally sided with the parents and did not back or support her new staff member. In fact, she wrote a letter on the sly and sent it downtown to a superintendent friend of hers. He proceeded to place it in a file without the knowledge of the parties concerned or a signature. Soon the assignment was completed, but there was little forthcoming work. We were wondering why this was occurring. Conlan knew there was a problem with some students but felt that it had been corrected. The administrator never gave him any reason to be concerned, just a brief session that something had been brought forward and taken care of.

When months had passed by, no more contract work was offered to him. During my days, I was waiting to hear some good news with great anticipation. I didn't want to get my hopes up but really couldn't help it. Each time I talked to Conlan, or the phone would ring, I would wonder if his turn had finally come. I grew more concerned as the time passed. Finally one day, I suggested that he go to the board office and see if there was a note or something placed in his file that he was not aware of. I don't know why I had such a strong hunch that something wasn't right. He went in to look at his file and found the letter that was written. It was horrible to read. It was untrue and terribly subjective. It said things like, "I feel that this young man should never be given a permanent position." There was no proof of any incidents or any true justification. The administrator just rambled on about personal thoughts and feelings. I couldn't believe how terrible it was that any administrator could do something like this without feeling guilt. Conlan had no choice but to bring the information forward to the union but he was not going to be successful. A dead end had been created for him no matter what he did. He would never be given a position now because he caught these supposed professionals in their unprofessional, callous way of working with people. They had been caught scheming but had the power to hide their ruthless little tricks. Needless to say, even though he fought the untrue allegations and they were removed, things actually did get worse.

Why does there have to be politics in everything? Yes, even in church and religion. I guess that maybe it's a popularity thing. Ever since the beginning of time, some people have competed to be recognized more than others. Our church was no exception. Everyone should be loved the same and treated equally, but that is never the case. The above mentioned administrator attends the same church as I do. Yes, the person that did all this damage to us put on a smile and set out to serve God and the church. How do you handle seeing someone be a Mass coordinator who has just proceeded to ruin a young life? Every time I would see the lady at Mass, I would return home with anger inside. The feeling kept growing and becoming more intense. Eventually it got to the point where I couldn't even look at her face. No guilt or remorse appeared apparent in her actions for behaving in a cruel way to another human being and I couldn't find a way to deal with my own feelings. It became so difficult after a while that I had to force myself to attend church because this person went to the same Mass as I did.

One Saturday, I was scheduled to be a Eucharistic Minister at the Mass I always attended. I generally arrived about ten or fifteen minutes before the scheduled deadline. All the Mass Coordinators know that I am reliable and show up early. The still practicing administrator happened to be the Mass Coordinator that night. When I walked in the Vestry to check my name off the list and print it on the white board, all the positions were filled. Other parishioners had arrived prior to me, and their offer to assist had been accepted even though I was scheduled to be there that night. Maybe she noticed that I was ignoring her. We had a somewhat negative past history so I could not begin to guess what had triggered this situation. Anyway, the coordinator looked at me and said, "I have enough help, you are not needed here." I could feel shock and possible tears that I would never begin to show, so I walked away. All I kept thinking through the whole Mass was, "maybe you're right. I am not needed here. I don't belong."

Upon leaving for home, Terry and I thought about all the terrible feelings we were dealing with in our family because of this person. Maybe we should get away for a while and go to another parish. I was really tired of holding in all this hurt and anger. I just wanted to leave. These people were a part of the hurt. The superintendent who had hid the letter attended our church and was credited for helping to build the new parish. I was constantly seeing people from the past that were upsetting to me. It seemed that searching for true Christian values was few and far between.

I mentioned earlier that the situation got even worse. Before the summer break, the superintendent had suggested to Conlan that he pursue a teaching position in another school system. The possible position didn't prove valid and was unsuccessful. We felt that it was a ploy to divert the past problem. The next year, he got a one year teaching contract in October which was to finish in June. The classroom was made up of grade seven and eight students. Conlan was given the class from hell. Apparently, the administrator at this school was not very effective either. There were serious problems that were not dealt with. The students knew that their disrespectful behaviour would be tolerated and had no fear of consequences. They were correct and would be very disruptive whenever they pleased. An attempt was being made for instruction but strong discipline was needed but not facilitated within the school setting.

Unfortunately, Conlan was becoming sick trying to deal with the problems in the classroom. One night, Sharla phoned and asked me to come over in the evening. When I saw him sitting on the sofa chair, I was afraid that he would die on the spot. I had never seen that much stress on a person's face. Conlan was pure white and I kept thinking that he wouldn't make it until morning. I had fear that he could even attempt suicide that night. I knew that I personally couldn't go back to the horrible situation that he was facing. I passed on all the encouragement that I could muster and could only suggest that he finish the year, while using his sick days for a break. God had to have carried him through to the finish.

I was praying that this time of our lives would come to an end. I prayed and asked and prayed and asked again. The answer from the Holy Spirit was not what I wanted to hear. I prayed during the day at work; I prayed when I came home. I prayed while preparing meals, and felt that God was not listening. He kept telling me to talk to our parish priest and not leave the church that I was attending. I had to leave that church because I couldn't bear to be there any longer. Whenever I had desperately prayed over the past number of years, God had answered and constantly surprised me. Why couldn't he do something like that this time too? Time was passing and nothing was getting achieved, in fact everything appeared to be moving in reverse. I could not even feel the presence of God at this point. Where was He when I needed Him most? It shouldn't take years to get your prayers decided one way or the other.

I knew that Conlan had to begin searching for another job because he couldn't spend another year without feeling success He eventually began a course in Adult Education from the university and we all hoped that it would lead to some new opportunities. God only continued to give me the one solution and I constantly rejected it. My serious prayers had begun with the substituting work for my son-in-law and my hopes were being dashed constantly. Tirelessly for the past approximately three years, I had been given the same answer over and over again.

I didn't want to speak to our parish priest. Father Steve had arrived in our parish about six years earlier. It took only casual observation to realize that he was going to be popular. Upon meeting him initially at the church, I noted that we lived only one house apart. That made it even more awkward to possibly confide my personal problems. Anyway, I was not going to tell or trust anyone. Nothing could be done about it. I had never really spoken to our priest except for polite conversation. What would I even say to him? He had to work with the people that I was experiencing difficulty with. Why should he even believe me? I could leave and go to another church. That way, at least I would get a break from the constant reminder of what was actually happening. I doubted that our parish priest even knew who I was, with all the people that he had to be responsible for. I would sneak away with my problems and not have to face them. At this point, the damage had been done so it wouldn't solve any problems to speak about them anyway.

Slowly during the time that the stress and sadness became more and more unbearable, Terry and I began to show up at Resurrection less often. Now that I had truly become involved in my church, I couldn't even consider not attending church services. It meant too much. Terry loved being with the music group 'Joyful Noise' at Holy Cross and they kept wanting us to return, so maybe this was a good time to make the move. Possibly, God was leading us back with all the negative things happening at Resurrection. I was thinking about leaving the ministries that I enjoyed because that would take some pressure off me, if I didn't care anyway. My vision became to sit in the back of the church as an obscure observer. Why did the message and strong feeling not go away? It kept telling me to go talk to a priest that I didn't really know. I would still be attending Mass and everybody at Holy Cross would be delighted that we had returned, so why did I feel that it was wrong? Why did I feel so terribly guilty? Terry was happy and actually registered us at Holy Cross. The priest there liked us and was pleased. After we had been gone for about three months, Terry thought it might be honest to inform Resurrection that we had switched parishes. People did it all the time.

All my prayer and uncertainty during such a long period of time, had led me to a kind of personal challenge. I believed that I was supposed to share my feelings and concerns with our parish priest who I didn't really know. I was given the feeling during my strong emotional prayer that if I didn't, he would come to talk to us. I thought this was my imagination and didn't believe it for a minute. We had barely exchanged a dozen significant words over the years and I didn't think that he really even knew who I was. Our church had more people than most others because everybody wanted to come there, and it was still growing. For me, that would be a reason to leave. I really didn't believe that our parish would miss two people when they already had so many. I was completely wrong because time would show that God had other plans for me. I should have followed my initial belief and shared my problems.

Our last Mass at Resurrection was in May. Over the summer, Terry and I had holidayed in Hawaii and I had pretty much forgotten most of my pain and anger. All problems seemed distant. I was becoming more relaxed at Holy Cross and never wanted to ever set foot in Resurrection again, I told myself. I didn't need the pain that seeing some of those people would recreate. Terry visited the church to inform them of our decision. The phone rang and Father Steve wanted to stop by and talk to us. Really!! I didn't think that was going to happen. I felt terribly uncomfortable. I knew that I would be honest because I'm not in the habit of lying and that wouldn't solve anything. It would probably feel good to let all that hurt go. I would try to maybe heal and move forward from this visit, but I wasn't going to change my mind and go back to all those insensitive people.

God always knows what's best and of course I should have listened. The most meaningful release of hurt occurred during that conversation. After having a talk and exploring some options, I finally felt that there were other choices. Father Steve made me feel that the problems could be dealt with and he offered us his support. I would have never believed how everything was almost instantly turned in a different direction. I began to feel that maybe I could face where I knew I wanted to be and belonged. We moved to our new church for a reason and had been a part of it since the very beginning. Father Steve mentioned something about running away. That would challenge me to return because I don't run away from anything. Now, what I was certain about a few days earlier was beginning to crumble. Plus, I was feeling guilty about resisting the Holy Spirit all those years. I had nothing to fear. Why did I begin to feel differently and that there was hope all along? I didn't reach out for it. As we were parting, I began to feel tears, and that is something that I never allow in front of anyone. Lucky Father Steve, he got me all tear-stained and sniffling as he left our house, but didn't seem to really mind.

I wrote Father Steve a thank you note and put it in his mailbox, but I had no intention of changing my mind. I remember sitting at my desk at the end of the school day, thinking that I still couldn't change what took me so many years to decide. I got used to my anger and hatred. I was not going to let them go that easy. We have made our final choice and were planning to stick with it. The Holy Spirit wasn't cooperating. Why did I feel this strong pull to return? No matter what I did it felt wrong and wouldn't go away. I was still basically miserable, even though I felt that everything should be settled. I should feel definite and secure, but I don't. I wanted more but just didn't know what. I felt like I was being torn in two different directions. Finally, I told Terry that I wanted to go to one more Mass at Resurrection to see what it felt like. Actually, it felt right again and the lady administrator wasn't even there.

Something else terribly strange was happening. Why did I want to go to Reconciliation? I hadn't gone for probably around twenty years and I never thought about it. All of a sudden, I felt an indescribable guilt that I hadn't quite experienced before. What was that all about? All I could think about was the many years that the Holy Spirit had attempted to guide me and I had deliberately disobeyed. At the time, I was absolutely sure that I was doing the right thing and that there was no other solution. Now, I felt that I disobeyed God and needed forgiveness for my lack of faith. I also wanted forgiveness for the hatred and anger that I had allowed into my life. I didn't want to carry that around with me any more or for years to come. It was amazing the number and variety of excuses that I had constructed to actually not face and run away from my problems.

CHAPTER 13:

combining God and church

Terry and I finally realized that we were attending Mass at Resurrection consistently again. We were also becoming involved in our ongoing ministries. I had signed up for proclaiming and Eucharistic ministries and was looking forward to moving and growing in my faith. Unbelievably, I no longer saw the administrator that was instrumental in my leaving in the first place. Since the time that I was seeing the people responsible for my unhappiness every Saturday evening, now I never encountered their presence except once in the distance. Why was this presence so apparent when I was trying to avoid the person and now that I felt a new strength they had disappeared? I couldn't help but wonder about the timing and purpose of this whole incident. I didn't realize that our absence actually impacted others in our faith community. Maybe I was being selfish in my own self-centered family concerns. People commented about how nice it was to see us at church again. We got more smiles and welcoming remarks than ever before and I felt a degree of guilt. I really did not wish to seek attention but now it seemed to be present. The passing of time helped to change that and soon our presence became routine again.

Several weeks after returning to Resurrection, the telephone rang on a Saturday afternoon. It was a couple of hours before Mass when I took the call. Feeling that I was once again fairly content and moving forward, the call caught me by surprise. The lady that coordinated the Rite of Christian Initiation for Adults requested the possibility of attending a meeting the following week. Apparently, a new woman had sought interest in our church and would need a possible sponsor. We could meet one afternoon and decide if we wished to pursue this outcome. My first reaction was that my calendar was already full with school work and my family. Terry was coaxing me to divert my negative feelings by allowing him to teach me to play the drums. I have no natural musical talent. That would be his challenge. He felt that it would be fun for me to learn something new. He was correct, except that I had to spend hours learning to keep the beat of a song while repeatedly listening to it. Years later, I can generally understand how to get a feel for the music. Eventually though, my interest subsided and practice was replaced by other interests.

The main interest that replaced my drum lessons was that I wanted to read the bible. I believed that the Holy Spirit (or God to my thinking) had generated all the things that had happened. It would be important for me to learn more about God. I thought the best place to begin was to read and learn as much as I could. The thought of reading the bible had crossed my mind previously, but when I began to analyze the amount of content, I always changed my mind. The pages were tissue paper thin. The amount of time to pursue this text would be endless. When I mentioned the possibility of this reading, people suggested a short and circuitous route to retain my interest throughout. I decided that with me the bible reading would be page by page starting from beginning to end. I eventually read the entire bible as I had originally set out to do. It was not a chore but became enjoyable. I used all available time to achieve my goal. Now, when I am a Mass Proclaimer words that appeared tough are not hard to pronounce. They make sense in the context of what is being read.

Saturday night Mass followed the telephone request. I had promised to contemplate the idea and return a phone call later on with my decision. At Mass, I continued to believe that nothing was more important than an opportunity to learn more about God and my faith. I wanted to become involved in my church even if it meant extra work and some late nights. I was pondering retirement at this point but was feeling it would happen in about three years. I had doubts about the time commitment but decided to say "yes" to be a sponsor. I actually found it difficult to believe that there wasn't a list of available people who wished to have this honour. I didn't suspect that I really needed any more time for my own faith. At that point, I had a strong, misunderstanding that because I had been a catholic, Christian person my entire life that I knew most of what I needed to know. Possibly, I could help another person with my knowledge. After church that evening I returned the phone call. I had already decided during the Mass to accept the offer.

I soon met the lady who was supposedly interested in becoming Catholic and anticipated the beginning of my new chance for involvement. During the time we spent together, I immediately noted the lack of content relating to God and church. She conversed in fluent English even though she was from another culture. The conversation was strange to me because I expected to be talking about my religion and not merely about school, family, children, and other general topics. I felt that maybe she didn't have enough insight to prepare and was keeping the time casual. I wanted her to be comfortable with me and relax. While visiting, I realized that there were ways that I could help her and her family because of my connections within the school system. I proceeded to assist with their needs as the first couple of months passed and we came to know each other better. She seemed to be a fantastic mother who was very loyal to her family and put their needs first. I admired her devotion.

Some of the early sessions had already begun when I arrived the first time. Most of the people had been introduced and already seemed to know each other. I was extremely nervous even walking to the church after supper. It was all completely new and something that I had never done before. When your life and schedule is already full of its many duties, having an opportunity to go to church wasn't practical. Allowing time to exercise and prepare for the next day following supper is what I had always allotted time for. Now, I was rushing to the church at night instead of only Saturday evening or Sunday morning. It felt very strange. I really didn't know about what people did in the evenings at the church. I totally didn't know what to expect.

The first session that I attended was a question and answers one. People had prepared questions during a previous session, so I just sat and listened. The lady that I was sponsoring sat beside me. She seemed very friendly and an awesome person. I was looking forward to the full year of sessions with her and to see how it would all unfold. Father Steve was leading and focusing on questions presented to him. At one point, he was talking about God as our creator. When he mentioned my name as an example of how we are each designed before birth, I felt really special in God's world for the first time. Yes, I talked to God but I never factored in creation. The world seemed too large for me to think that God knew me personally. I mentioned earlier how I believed that I was always lost in the crowd, whether it was at school, at church, or in the world. I never felt that I was created uniquely by God and that there was a real purpose for my life. I felt that I just was and that things happened. I couldn't control things but I could always ask for God's help and He allowed me to follow the course of His plans. Going home, pondering this new thinking began to change the way that I thought about myself. It seemed unreal that God had actually created me special and not as in an insignificant group. How could He keep track of all His creation with a whole world of people and places, over all time?

The following sessions were just as interesting. We learned about the parts of the Mass and the vestments that the priest wore on special occasions. We became familiar with the instruments of celebration used during the Mass and their names. Some sessions included the church year calendar, the seven sacraments were looked at separately and their purpose, the overview of the bible, the saints, special feast days celebrated, and many fascinating items. Even though I had been a Catholic since birth, there was so much that I didn't know. I realized how much I was hungering for all this knowledge. Sometimes, there was a special Mass or blessing for the group which was beautiful beyond words. It seemed though, that my hunger for knowledge was not what my new Inquirer was experiencing. She was failing to show up at many of the sessions and I felt strange sitting alone with nobody to really sponsor. The day that they were to be introduced and recognized at the Mass, she showed up late and I was unsure of what to do. It was a horrible, uncomfortable feeling that made me wonder how serious this lady really was. I was also asked to help her learn about 'Who Jesus is," by viewing some tapes from the Alpha program but it seemed she was never available to get together. She would often cancel or postpone our visits with various excuses. When we did manage to get together, she would always need me to repeat the information that had just been viewed. When we reviewed and discussed the material, she would act like she had little to no understanding. I was dreading not attending the sessions now that I wanted and needed to continue, but I didn't see the point of being a sponsor with nobody to sponsor.

When the lady that I was sponsoring began to not show up frequently, I decided to speak to Father Steve about my concerns. If she didn't show up the one night, I had committed myself to actually telling about my prompting visits. With the greatest fear that I have ever known in a long time, I decided to be honest and tell how God has been involved in my life already. While I had been dealing with my earlier mentioned problems, I had known that the time would come that I could no longer keep my relationship to God as my own secret. I had to begin by telling someone else as it was intended to happen. With my fear in check, I decided that a priest could be a good place to start. I asked Father Steve if we could have a few moments to speak. I would tell him my concerns about continuing in the program. He said that I should continue until Christmas and we would see what happens until then. I swallowed all my pride and fears. Shakily, I stated that I believed Jesus had been guiding me to this point. I can't even imagine his full thoughts when I spoke this way. Each time I said that Jesus was directing me; he corrected me to 'the Holy Spirit'. I kind of ignored him because I had no knowledge of the Holy Spirit. The Spirit was a total, foreign entity to me. I related to God as the creator of the world and I related to Jesus because He lived in a human form, but the Holy Spirit didn't fit into anything that I knew. Ironically, the Holy Spirit was with me during all that time and I didn't know it. After our discussion, I felt better that I had actually spoken of what I believed had happened. I told Father about being guided to come speak with him but being too afraid. I mentioned how it had gone on for many years. I was so nervous and uncomfortable about everything that I'm sure what he heard was very strange. Anyway, I had taken the first step and that's what counted. I had given up talking to Terry and my children about some of my spiritual encounters years earlier, so maybe finally opening up and being honest would prove my accountability to God.

I could feel that it would happen, and it eventually came true. The lady that I was sponsoring decided to not follow through with the program and I felt compelled to leave. There was no real purpose to attend with nobody to sponsor. I thought I would now have free time in the evenings to enjoy for myself. I was wrong again. Instead of being happy and relieved, I found myself missing the learning and the people, but I never said anything. Maybe it was meant to happen that way. It was not unusual for my first try at different things to go wrong, that appeared to be the story of my life. It happened to me all the time. It was great to still be involved in my ministries, and I knew that I would have really missed them. Terry became involved in music at the church again. Often we would attend a couple of Masses. Terry would come if I was scheduled for a Saturday Mass and I would go on Sunday if he was scheduled to play the drums with the Folk group. We usually attended another Mass at Holy Cross when Terry played the drums with Joyful

Noise. He loved the people and the group far too much and needed to belong. I didn't mind being at Mass often now that I understood the parts and their meaning. Mass actually went very quickly while before it seemed to drag.

The following summer before the Saturday evening Mass, I asked Father Steve if I could possibly sponsor another person since I never had the chance to go through the whole program. He listened to me and nodded with assent. I believed that he would allow me the opportunity. I have a strong need to feel that something I undertake achieves full fruition. There is the greatest sense of accomplishment to see undertakings come to an end.

CHAPTER 14:

my journey in faith

When autumn arrived, it was time for RCIA to begin again. This time I was excited and hoping to sponsor someone who actually desired to become a Catholic. I have faith and much to offer that person, I believe. It was great to be welcomed at the first phase of the Rite of Christian Initiation for Adults journey and attend the Alpha course. I had already witnessed the course once with Conlan and so this was a repeat. I initially found the course interesting but felt that I already had a personal relationship with God. I didn't care for the Praise and Worship music and failed to see everyone else's enthusiasm for it at that point. Ironically, a couple of years later, I became totally enthralled with this style of music. There was a purpose for taking Alpha again and so it felt valuable and worthwhile. One evening at the session, I encountered a lady that had an interest in becoming Catholic. I learned later on that I would get to sponsor her and was truly thrilled. This experience proved to be entirely different. It was positive and growing. I soon knew and felt that I would manage to accomplish what I had failed to do the first time. The really neat and special thing was that this amazing lady already had faith. She was open to God and His word. She wanted to grow, learn, and become a Catholic for her family. I truly hoped that I could inspire her that God is real and that she should never quit or give up on her faith.

Upon the completion of the Alpha course there was a date set aside for a retreat weekend. The retreat was to be held in the Qu'Appelle valley during November. We drove out to the destination in a group. Retreat experiences are always generally beautiful times and this one was amazing. The time was spent in prayer, presentations, and discussions, meditating, and socializing, especially at meal times. The lady that I was sponsoring involved herself in everything offered. It was a blessing to be forming a bond of friendship. She confided that the weekend was very meaningful to her faith journey. I was pleased to feel a part of her joy.

I fully considered this my time of learning my faith. Maybe it had something to do with repeating many of the sessions. I found that much was being internalized since I had learned many things for the first time and now I could feel it solidly within. I also had past history to draw on and so the information was making more sense. I was actually incorporating much of my faith into my life. It was a new understanding added on with the experience and belief of the past. I think that God was providing for a new addition to my life. I always had general knowledge and history of the church. It was the time of Mass in Latin, memorizing catechism, and the much needed change. Without the awesome way in which we celebrate the Mass today, I would have probably become distant and not as involved as I am at the present time. I have a strong desire to pursue much more and not be content with merely participating on a Sunday.

A special meaningful event happened that year during early spring. The church was preparing for the Easter season and was beginning with the Lenten observances. During this time, the Stations of the Cross were celebrated every Friday evening. I had participated once at Holy Cross parish by doing some of the readings, but that was several years earlier. When the e-mail was sent out from the parish office for people to assist, I wanted to become involved. I answered the request and was given the chance to participate for the first evening. I was to carry the cross and stand at each station. It seemed to me that the other people present may have had opportunities to assist with evening celebrations and knew what to do. When I arrived, I wasn't offered any instruction. I was embarrassed by my lack of knowledge. Anyway, I survived after asking questions. Of course, now I know the procedure and would not hesitate to aid a new person. The lack of knowledge was quite intimidating and if I was insecure and not stubborn, I would have probably never offered again. I would have been an observer and not a participant.

The second special religious event happened a few weeks later. I was given the rare opportunity to participate at the Holy Thursday Mass by having my feet washed. The blessings were happening too quickly for me to feel anything but awe. I was getting attention from the church that I wasn't used to. Just being a part of the Stations of the Cross made me feel unbelievable but now to add another request was more than I could describe in words. Of course I would say 'Yes'. I had to work at school all day Thursday but made sure that I was prepared when the evening came. The experience was incredibly humbling and one that I will never forget. I can see why Jesus would have washed his apostle's feet since it created a very strong feeling that could never be changed or erased. Once you have participated there is no way that you wouldn't remember it or have it change your life. The feeling of humility is beyond belief. Whenever a person mentions that they had their feet washed, they always relate how humble they felt afterwards. I know that I will never forget it.

Terry and I had been very busy at that time sending out invitations for our 40th Wedding anniversary which was coming in June. We initially desired a house party. We discovered that there were going to be more people invited than our home could accommodate. The final decision leads us to our church community. Father Steve had mentioned that we could renew our wedding vows and that would be amazing. I was feeling special that we could be remarried, in a sense, during a Mass and not just have people present for the taking of vows. The Mass would be at five o'clock on Saturday, June 8th and our actual wedding took place on Saturday, June 9th, 1973, which was the next day, the Sunday. It was extremely close to the exact date. We were also lucky to have beautiful weather for both of the above mentioned dates. It drizzled slightly during the afternoon of our 40th anniversary. Ironically, the rainy mist completely stopped as I had to carry the cake into the church hall. It started up again right after. I hope that God was once again smiling down on us. People told us afterwards that the church was packed for that evening and some had to leave. They said that they didn't mind when they realized what was happening and were happy for us. One lady said that hearing us say the vows brought tears to her eyes. I only knew that I was standing with the man who I loved the most in the world and we belonged together always.

Soon, the new school year began and I realized that this would be the final one until I retire. I knew I would be participating in the celebration of twenty-five teaching years at the opening Mass. I didn't want all the exciting events to overlap so I intended to teach for twenty-six years. I would continue teaching one year past twenty-five, because I didn't think the events would be enjoyable if I had to rush from planning one thing to another. I decided to space them and really enjoy them all.

The opening Mass was at Resurrection for the first time. With the new church now open, it could accommodate the large numbers of staff that the cathedral was having trouble with. At the cathedral, many people would be standing through the Mass and speeches that followed. It was really hot and cramped in that building as well. Parking was an issue at the cathedral and Resurrection had more space. I was thrilled to be getting my twenty-five year recognition at my home parish. I didn't even have to bother taking my car or worry about parking. I could walk there. When I arrived at the church, I wasn't afraid to sit close to the front since it was a comfortable space where I sat during RCIA. After the Mass, we were called up to the Sanctuary steps for a group photo. Then we received a beautiful Wilf Perrault painting depicting a Regina back alley scene. Even though it was large and cumbersome, I managed to carry it home from the church.

The students at the school knew that this was my final year of teaching before retirement and were being needier than in the past. I was getting far more attention, love and hugs than I was used to. The final year of teaching and RCIA fully coincided and would both end at the same time. I had this terrible fear of letting go, and really dreaded the end of the year even though it was inevitable. The library volunteer students were doing everything in their power to make me feel special and showing that they would miss me.

A positive staff incentive was introduced at the retreat early in the school year. Many of the teachers were being recognized later at the school for various things that they had done. The library volunteer girls felt that it wasn't fair that I hadn't been recognized so they created a beautiful certificate for me. It was far more meaningful than the actual one given by the office because it was drawn, coloured, labeled and laminated by the girls themselves. What a fantastic treasure that I proudly displayed on the wall in the library. I remember how excited and pleased they were to present it to me. Those are the special moments that I would find difficult to leave behind. Experiences like this come from working with children and are rarely found anywhere else.

I was now participating again in the second year of RCIA by being a sponsor; I was beginning to feel comfortable at church. By being at the front in many special events, parishioners were recognizing me and making comments. It was unsettling because it felt unfamiliar. Being noticed and loved by the children at school is natural because you spend your days teaching and caring for them which can create a special bond. Church participation and recognition was still fairly new to me and I preferred to be one of the many.

Contentedly involved in the Rite of Christian Initiation of Adults, I felt that speaking of my messages on a couple of opportunities to Father Steve and participating in learning, had moved me to what God's intent truly was. There was much more to my learning and growth than I had ever imagined. I had been more of an observer than a participant. During the second year of the RCIA journey, I got a series of special opportunities that would change my life and entrench my faith even deeper. Thinking that I already had a deep knowledge of my faith and church, I had no idea that there was so much more for me to learn. This special time and process will probably remain a favourite time of my life. After teaching for years, it was wholesome and healthy to be learning again. What better topic could I find than the God who I had been speaking to and seeking all along?

I had noticed from the previous participants in RCIA that there would be opportunities in the second year to do readings and provide more knowledge about being a Catholic and Christian my whole life. The sessions began with Growing Faith and meeting at the homes of people who were participating. We were a fairly large group and I hosted an evening only once. The weeks spent witnessing this part of the journey were more personal and helped to build community. The Sunday Masses leading up to Easter were reserved for the Scrutinies. Our group of people really became comfortable and most of us completed the two years together.

When the new Ministry schedule was delivered, leading up to Easter. I noticed that my name was listed for being a Reader at the Passion on Palm Sunday. Once again, this was brand new to me. Anticipation had become a part of that particular day because I was to be sharing in something that I had only watched from a seat and never had an opportunity to do. Being nervous was not a huge problem, even though it set me slightly back, but also presented the challenge which I loved. I was sent the words of the reading and they weren't difficult. Besides, I had been teaching, presenting, and proclaiming for many years already and this was my opportunity.

One day soon after receiving the ministry schedule, I was driving home from school. There was still snow on the ground so I was being cautious. I was listening to one of my favourite CD's. While driving, my mind was mulling over everything that was upcoming in the near future. I realized that after Easter many exciting things would be happening for me with the culmination of RCIA and my teaching career. I contemplated all these events. Instantaneously, an unexplained flash of knowing entered my mind that I would be reading at the Easter Vigil. I hadn't had any spiritual messages for some time and this one caught me by surprise. I immediately discarded it as thinking too much about the future. It went away after I got home and I soon forgot about it. The following week, when I was driving home from school, I got the same message that I would be reading at the Easter Vigil. On this trip home, I felt that it was Friday and therefore my mind must be tired. Strangely, it was the same message as before. The message seemed to be persisting like the one that told me to talk to Father Steve after the teaching/school problems. It could have been just my mind thinking about the only remaining special event that I could possibly be a reader at. I may have been wishing that it was so. I forgot about it over the weekend again; totally putting it out of my mind. As the weeks went by, the message kept repeating and persisting as I drove home from school. Realizing that the Easter season was fast approaching, I knew that soon I would discover if my message was for real or not.

It was the end of the day on Wednesday and I was driving home from school. It was also the night of RCIA and I was thinking about supper and getting ready. As I was driving, the message reappeared. It said, "You will be asked to read at the Easter Vigil." I did the usual denial, feeling that because I had been scheduled as a Passion Proclaimer that I would not be asked to do another special reading. It occurred to me that if I was to be requested it would have to be soon. I would know for sure if my message was real or not. I believed that the feeling would soon disappear and I would realize it for just being a possible idea that had entered my mind. At seven o'clock I arrived at the church and we were sitting in a circle of chairs. The lady that I was sponsoring was sitting beside me. Before we began the evening, the Pastoral Assistant approached me and asked if I would be willing to read at the Easter Vigil. The unexpected feeling of surprise was amazing. I said that I would be honoured to as I thought about my earlier messages. No matter how often the messages happen, they can't be predicted and totally are a surprise. I honestly froze at the moment. It was beyond belief that I had been repeatedly told about being asked and now it had happened. As Father Steve walked by in the hallway, I had the urge to run out the door and state, "you will never believe what just happened?" I knew that it would be embarrassing to both of us so I just sat with a strange, numb feeling of disbelief.

That Easter, I did experience reading at the Vigil. The meaning of what was happening was wonderful. There was one problem. The night of Holy Thursday, I felt like I was beginning to experience soreness in my throat. Good Friday, I felt my throat was sore but thought maybe it would still disappear with the right medication. Sadly, during the Saturday, my throat became worse and I was beginning to lose my voice. By Saturday evening, my voice sounded quiet and croaky. How was I going to read in front of a packed church with an inaudible voice? It was too late to find a replacement. Plus, the lady that I was sponsoring all these past years needed me to be present. I prayed all day. At night, I was still quite sick but managed to do my reading. I was disappointed thinking of how I probably sounded but felt that at only one point was I hard to understand. I truly did my best. Maybe this was meant to be a time of humility.

During the Easter holiday, we flew to Victoria, B.C for a short visit. I kept getting a premonition. I kept feeling that I was at Resurrection church and a casket was placed in front of the altar. I kept getting a strong feeling that I was passing out the Eucharist to people from our school system. Will I be asked as a Eucharist minister at the opening school Mass? My feeling was that the two messages were not related. I also wondered what these feelings had to do with me. During the summer that followed, I was asked to be a Eucharistic minister for a young Administrative assistant who passed away quickly and unexpectedly. Many of the people that I served were from the school system. There was also the casket in front of the altar. I could feel all the feelings explained from my knowing and they disappeared when I went home.

When school resumed after Easter, I was now in the home stretch. I had many wonderful celebrations to mark my upcoming retirement.

The first big surprise was when the students in the library book club gave me a retirement lunch in the multi-purpose room. Noon hour had just begun and I was walking to the staff room to eat my bag lunch. The vice-principal stopped me in the hallway and mentioned that some students were waiting for me. She stated that my lunch was not necessary because they had ordered a pizza. When I got to the room all the students were waiting. It was beautiful because they had organized everything. I was presented a large bouquet of red roses. After the pizza lunch, the children read messages that they had written themselves. They were the most meaningful words that came straight from the heart. I was extremely moved by the way in which the afternoon was prepared. We also enjoyed a decorated chocolate cake. The cake and flowers were my favourite ones of course.

A strange turn of events happened one day during this joyous time. It was now moving towards the end of May. Retirement fun was always in the back of my mind but there was much work that needed attending to before that happened. My mind was constantly occupied. The day began overcast, drizzly, and eventually the weather turned into rain. I was expecting a couple of visitors to the library. They were to help me organize and delete what needed more professional decision making. That particular afternoon was very light-hearted and fun. We were jokingly tossing old books around and chatting amongst the shelves. When I glanced over at one of the ladies, I had a premonition of her being covered in grit, like being in a windy dust storm. My mind absorbed the thought that she would die in a few months. I tried to turn the thought away as quickly as possible. All I could think was, "what a horrible thing to think about somebody. I'm going to focus on happiness because my mind is playing tricks with the gloominess of the day and the fact that I won't be working here next year." As the afternoon wore on, I initiated a variety of interesting topics such as upcoming holidays and all the new retirees that year. Sadly, that horrible thought continued to reoccur and could not be shaken.

I walked into the hallway with the remaining lady, since the other one had to leave a little earlier. The battling process became more profound. I kept fighting the thought of whether to pass on the information and tell her or not. My mind kept replaying, "Whenever you feel something this strong, you know that it always comes true." How can you possibly inform somebody of impending misfortune? I hurt inside with the wrenching struggle going on. Time was running out and she was now at the outside door. Do I say a warning–but how-or just let her walk away not knowing anything? The inner torment led to tears beginning to trickle down my cheek. I was beginning to sniffle with embarrassment. I fabricated the excuse about having seasonal allergies. As she began to exit the door, I felt painfully helpless and glad that this would soon be over. All I could say to her was, "I really enjoyed spending the afternoon with you. Take real good care of yourself." She turned back at me laughing and responded, "I always do." The door closed and she was gone. Turning back down the hallway, I stopped at the staff washroom because I had begun to cry uncontrollably by this point. As I looked in the mirror, I tried giving myself a pep talk. First, I tried to realize that this wasn't necessarily real and it was totally strange that I would be feeling this way. What was going on? Why would I get this type of information? We were only casual friends and didn't know each other very well. Where did this information come from, and why to ME? I concentrated on calming myself with the assurance that my mind had created this and was really just working overtime. Nobody needed to know how ridiculous I was being right now. I could keep it to myself forever, since it was just my fabrication and not real at all. I reached for the doorknob and stopped myself to ensure that people passing by don't see me as the wreck I am. They would probably question me about what was the matter since my eyes were red and puffy. Aren't I dumb crying over something unreal that should never really happen? I say, "God, please let this stay in my mind. I don't want it to come true and happen, but if it does, I will never doubt that you are responsible and wanted all those things to happen to me in the past. This is just too strange and I should never doubt you after knowing this." Time soon passed with all the upcoming events, and that day faded into a memory of the past.

Retirement proceeded as I had requested it should happen. For me, it was all about the children and staff that I worked with. I didn't want any large production. I wanted a special day at school with the same people that I spent every day with. The day began with a surprise breakfast in the library. I was given a corsage and the tables were decorated. My chair had balloons and ribbons attached. There were fun Jeopardy games and laughter as the meal progressed. To me, it was the greatest to hear the laughter and have fun with the staff. After lunch, there was a special assembly in the gym. The entire school was there to send me off. Each class did something unique, either a poem or short story, and presented me with a yellow rose until I had a full bouquet. I could feel the room full of cheering and laughing. It was amazing beyond words. I treasure those simple, meaningful momemts of love.

All new retirees were recognized at the Hotel Saskatchewan for their superannuation. It was a wonderful evening with a program, wine and cheese, etc. Each retiree had to write a short autobiography about themselves. I mentioned how I wished to continue into the future by substitute teaching and taking a larger role in my church community. The retirees were again recognized at the Hotel Saskatchewan by the School Board. The program was used for the second time based on the short autobiographical sketches. This time it had little sayings under everybody's names. Immediately when I opened the program and read the comments under the names, I noticed that they mentioned various notations of retirement. My random program quote was, "We may ignore, but we can nowhere evade, the presence of God. The world is crowded with him. He walks everywhere incognito." – C.S. Lewis. I am thrilled that my love and belief in God had been assigned at such a special event. What a wonderful coincidence. It is exactly what I feel and what has been happening in my life.

CHAPTER 15:

endings and new beginnings

It seemed strange that all the busy events had now come to an end. RCIA was completed in early June with special evenings and retreats. It was a truly fantastic time of spiritual learning and growing. I was now retired from teaching and felt insecure about what the future would include. Most of all, my personal spiritual happenings were weighing on my mind. Everything may have felt more frightening because I was tired and worn from the busy schedule, excitement, and excessive amount of attention. It was amazing the amount of energy that was lost when the school year was finally over and I personally felt drained. The job of teaching is rewarding but a person feels exhausted for several weeks after the end. Now, I really needed time alone to ponder and sort out my life again. I would have to recreate what I do since it won't be scheduled and organized as it had been in the past.

I decided that I would begin by reaffirming my desire to find God's destiny for me. I would not let fear prevent me from dealing with something so important. I still found it difficult to tell Father Steve about my spiritual messages and visits. By keeping them inside, I wasn't accountable to others about what was happening. I really didn't want to tell and generally fought it all the way. My excuses didn't win out. When I finally had admitted that I was supposed to be open about my spirituality, it felt surreal but very honest. I had arranged a second visit with Father Steve during RCIA. I knew now that God had moved me to accountability. There was no more hiding. He wanted me to make known His gift and wonder. I was content being me and not someone with special visits in the past. I was afraid and shaking again as I went to tell Father about the more recent events. He looked like he believed me but didn't know quite what to make of it. He was kind and listened politely but I felt that maybe he was being too professional. I really also had to thank him for all the opportunities that had come to me and knew that he had to have done some arranging in that regard. I needed to say how much it meant to renew our vows at the anniversary and do the readings. He just listened and acknowledged. I still had some work to do if I was to be believed completely.

How does someone behave that has just revealed their most inner-most self to another person? I was full of doubt. I really didn't want to change and worry about all those Christian ideals that were slowly becoming revealed and known. I liked being obscure and just another parishioner. The show of appreciation was extremely important but even past that moment; I wanted to go back. That probably wasn't meant to be. I felt that maybe my visits and short discussions with Father Steve were meant to stop. He was really busy without me taking up his valuable time. As I walked towards home after my late June visit, I felt that I really had to prove myself in a much more extreme way if this was the path that I wished to pursue. Maybe it was time for that to happen. Instead of feeling that I would be more involved in the church and faith, I felt that the opposite was happening. I walked into the parish office looking for something motivational and inspirational. When I left, even though I'm sure it wasn't intended, I felt uncertain. It hurt and upset me whether I misunderstood the intent or not. I still felt the encounter as a questionable experience and didn't feel any future direction. Are you opening my eyes more towards you God and leading me back into humility after the revelations and experiences? You could be teaching me another lesson through my doubt and pain. God in my life is real and always has been is something that I needed to remember. I could never deny it and be honest. There are just too many things that have happened.

It was now the middle of July, 2014 and I had been falling asleep feeling very tired and sensitive to people and what they say. This particular night, I had gone to bed still exhausted. Suddenly, I was awakened from my deep sleep around three o'clock in the morning. There was a sensation of some men having a discussion outdoors under my bedroom window. The voices were muffled. A voice, with no voice that could be easily understood, unfolded to me a message that my half asleep brain tried to interpret. "Anything you do for God is good." The mention of God created sparks of excitement at that particular moment. I could feel my pulse quicken. My mind tried to make sense of the message. I was certain that I would not be able to remember what was said when I woke up in the morning. Almost immediately my mind perceived an obscure book page that was open. I could plainly see where the pages divided along the spine. There was a soft glow of yellow and pastel green surrounding the outside of the book. I felt someone or something looking over my shoulder and instructing me, just like a teacher would assist a student having difficulty with a problem. Gently, I was guided by a finger image to see the page separation and the word 'anything' divided in half. The word 'any' is on one page and 'thing' is on the other page in large print. Next came the word 'you' on one page and 'do' on the opposite page side. The remaining words were distributed in the same way. 'For' was written on one page and 'God' on the opposite side. 'Is' and 'good' are written exactly the same way.

I know that with this word presentation, I will certainly remember it forever. These words will become my lifelong motto. I wished to try and decipher the message in my now totally awake mind. First, I think that 'anything' may be easily misinterpreted. Many people murder and say that voices or even God told them to do it. The word 'you' can be either singular or plural. Is the message relating specifically to me or to people in general? I felt unexplained restlessness with this line of thinking. My mind really couldn't seem to make sense of this. I continued trying to figure out what was said without success. With much frustration, I decided that if we try our hardest to do God's will that God will be pleased. I could continue trying to interpret this message for the rest of my life. My mind now relaxed and I fell back into a deep sleep. It felt like mere minutes when morning had arrived and I woke up once again. It was now seven o'clock and a beautiful, bright sunshine was entering the bedroom. I quickly sat up and had the memory foremost in my mind. What had happened last night? Should I believe that it was real? Then I reminded myself that I was wide awake at that point in the night. How did morning come so quickly with total recall of all events in my mind? I have had many messages in promptings and dreams over the years, but I have never had something so realistic happen to me. Could I ever deny it if I was forced to take a lie-detector test or someone was pointing a gun at me? The answer is no. I could not deny that I was given a special visit and I still need to make sense of what actually is intended of me. I know that part of the message related to me not attempting to control my life and everything in it. I am to let God have control. I should be trusting in Him.

I couldn't help but tell Terry about the vision the next morning, after being very apprehensive. Every time that I had mentioned spiritual visits to him, he appeared completely skeptical. I had to approach this revealing in the correct fashion. I needed to tell somebody and knew that I didn't wish to return to the parish office. Terry was sitting out on our enclosed deck drinking his coffee and reading the newspaper. As I spoke to him, Terry realized that I was completely serious and needed to be believed. He commented that I was lucky and he wished that something that great would happen to him but probably never would. I couldn't impress upon him enough how great the wonder and beauty had been.

The music group 'VISION' was completing the work they had begun recording a CD called 'Reverence'. Terry had to drive to Strasbourg one evening for a sound check. I decided to drive out with him for the short visit. When we arrived, Terry and Dave went up to the studio. Carole was out on her deck watching the sunset. The panorama of big sky and colour was beautiful on the lake as we leaned over the deck to observe. Silently, as if not to break the spell of the moment, we began to converse. As the sky darkened and the bugs thickened, we decided to eventually move indoors. Carole instantly made me feel comfortable as she related possibly beginning an Alpha course in their home town. She had led many groups and was extremely knowledgeable and confident in her faith. She continued to relate how the Holy Spirit would move her to be certain if the time was right. It was at that point that I felt maybe this was a good time to tell another person about my vision and gauge her reaction. She believed me instantly. Carole felt comfortable talking to me about the Holy Spirit. We conversed about all aspects of the vision. She felt that I was being asked to do something that would be extremely difficult. I should persevere no matter how difficult everything may seem at the time. Carole prophesized that for the following year, I would feel alone and deserted by everybody. It would be one of the worst years of my life. The year would also be the most worthwhile one in the service to God. She was very serious and adamant.

I still needed to know more about my vision so I persuaded Terry to visit Pastor Paul Gosselin, who is my nephew, but also a Pentecostal minister. Their children are still very young and so I spoke openly about what happened during my night vision. We had a great visit. Paul made me feel content about confiding in him. We have a lifelong comfort level of knowing each other. He was comfortable talking about the Holy Spirit visiting. We relaxed and discussed God and Scripture all afternoon. After a lovely evening meal, it was time to leave for Regina. I was absolutely content and pleased that I had come to visit him. I left feeling that what had happened was not really that unusual because God speaks to us quite often. It is up to us to recognize when and how He is communicating to us. All too soon, we were proceeding to the door with many hugs and promises to see each other. Alanna, Pastor Paul's wife, stopped me at the door to wait for a minute. She appeared with a large, paperback book in her hand. The novel was called 'The Chronicles of Narnia' by C. S. Lewis. She impressed on me the importance of how I should pay attention to the lion character 'Aslan' since he reflects the presence of God in the story. Alanna assured me that I don't have to stress over reading the book immediately since it is hers. She was not in a hurry to have it returned soon. I told her that I would read it soon anyway.

In August, the music group 'VISION' was asked to play at Rock the Mount. It is a one day event that is well prepared and attended annually. Terry and I packed and prepared to join the group in Humboldt. We would be staying at St. Peter's Abbey in Muenster. It was our second consecutive year of participation in this special Praise and Worship event. The first year featured the saints and actually had actors dressed in costumes and telling their stories. There was a special presenter, the stations of the cross, Reconciliation, a candlelight vigil, and a Mass. The day was full of music and activity. The second year was set up much the same as the first one was. This year, the keynote speaker was Sister Miriam James Heidland. She is from Texas and has an amazingly vibrant personality. I really enjoyed listening to her present. Sister was captivating and the audience was enthralled with her message. I immediately noted that her speech was paralleling her life with characters from 'The Chronicles of Narnia'. Was it a coincidence that Alanna had given me that book at random to read just a few weeks earlier? What are the chances that such an unexpected match would occur?

The following morning, after having spent the night at the Abbey, we got ready and went for breakfast. Terry and I ended up eating and visiting with a new VISION musician and his wife. Meanwhile, another couple from the group was privileged to be sitting at the table with Sr. Miriam and enjoying her company. When we prepared to leave back for Regina, we stopped in the other dining room. Sr. was visiting with another lady, Lori, the leader of the group's wife. When I approached the table, Lori asked me if I would be interested in doing a bible study with her based on Sister's new book. Her book entitled 'Loved as I Am' was to be released for purchase around Christmas time. Lori and I both realized that it would benefit us to read 'The Chronicles of Narnia.' I was delighted to be asked to do my first bible study cooperatively with a friend. I decided to read the book while I was holidaying in September. I stipulated to Lori that I had volunteered to possibly help with RCIA at Resurrection and would do the bible study with her if I wasn't needed there.

September seemed a good time to get away. With the new school year starting, I knew that I would miss everybody too much. It would be too hard to not be a part of school events. Terry and I decided to take our summer vacation in September and therefore, we would be out of town and away from all the activity. We began our vacation in Old Quebec. It gave us a good sample of what life was like in Canada many years ago. There was an enormous Cathedral mere blocks from our hotel. The building occupied an entire city block. It was built out of huge bricks but unfortunately due to the cost of maintenance large sections of the lower level was set up as private businesses. We attended Mass there on the Sunday and didn't understand very much of it. It was all spoken in French. After a week of touring the Upper and Lower Quebec village in the historic district, we moved on to Montreal using Via Rail.

Tuesday we arrived in Montreal. We once again had to orient ourselves. All morning we visited a variety of shopping malls. I was excited about all the new stores we don't have in Regina. Shopping was great and the deals were amazing. In the afternoon, we returned to our hotel and rested for a while. We decided to check out the huge 'Basilique Cathedrale Marie-Reine-du-Monde' or 'Mary, Queen of the World' Basilica and Cathedral. We had seen the building on the way to our hotel from the Via Rail Station on the first day. After the breathtaking stroll around the building, we returned to the entrance. There we noticed a little gift shop. I was looking for a special present for a teacher friend of mine. The selection was exquisite and I found what I needed pretty quickly. The final choice was difficult though. As I went to pay for my purchases, the lady in the shop started chatting with me. I remarked about my years of teaching and recent retirement. She looked at me and commented, "I see much love in your eyes. Perhaps, God is calling you to do a different job for Him now." I felt immediate connection with what she had said.

The next day started like any other day on our vacation. For some odd reason, I felt that God was very distant today. We were going to be walking about five miles to see the Montreal St. Joseph's Oratory. The road there was mostly all uphill. The sun was extremely hot and we didn't want to drink much water because there were no washroom facilities along the route. The big churches in Montreal had been beautiful and impressive, but not personally meaningful. When we finally arrived at the Oratory, I was already tired and my feet were sore. There were hundreds of stairs to climb but, we finally arrived at the entrance. In the Information Hall, there was a paper, stand-up of Brother Andre. I could feel his eyes on me and his very presence. I paid little heed and continued on with the tour. The building outside was very majestic but the interior appeared simple to me. When we walked to the burial tomb and later the room depicting Brother Andre's death and heart, the full impact struck home. I was in the presence of a real saint. I could feel him telling me to be unique and do what God is asking, just like he did. I must follow my own path. I do have a special purpose given by God but not totally discovered as yet. I could feel immense emotion within that I could hardly contain without tears.

The last week of our September getaway was in Ottawa. Our national capital is a very beautiful city. We desperately wanted to view the Parliament Buildings. When we arrived in Ottawa that was one of the first things we decided to do. Strangely coincidental was the fact that we stood at the exact spot where a shooting occurred one month later to the hour and day. The horrible newsworthy event happened in October in the large hallway of the building. Terry and I were glad that the gunman wasn't there in September. He should have never decided to shoot a ceremonial guard in front of the war memorial. We were sad that the terrible incident had happened.

Upon returning to Regina, I wanted to be involved in the school system again because I truly missed the students and staff. I needed to still feel a part of what was happening, even though it was already in progress. A dear teacher friend of mine, Gwen, allowed me to volunteer in her grade one classroom. I loved being with her students. I didn't feel as left out after that. Soon, the phone began to ring and I started getting requested for substitute teaching. I know that teaching is still my passion and probably will always remain. Time is once again passing and life feels on track.

The feeling that something really important is still missing soon becomes very strong to me. The Holy Spirit prompts me to go to Reconciliation and I feel compelled to talk about my summer vision. I am searching for some feedback while strongly realizing that there is no true explanation. I need Father Steve to know that what I have been telling him is real. It won't change anything. There is just too much history already but maybe stating my facts during confession will definitely validate them. I had watched a video relating how God doesn't work in our lives by repeating His expectations. Why is there constant repetition that I feel compelled to struggle with? For a reason that I can't explain it is important that I am believed. Now, I strongly feel that the Holy Spirit is pulling me towards accountability and I have to write about God in My Life. It is time to tell about his wonders and all that has happened. I begin to write this book and believe that it is intended. It feels right. Every time that I feel doubt about the value in writing this account of my life in a book, I end up changing my thinking and desire to continue. I keep remembering that 'Anything you do for God is good.'

Early in January, I had a dream that I was at an outdoor banquet. There were endless varieties of foods of all kinds. They are displayed in tents on beautiful dishes. People started taking the large dinner plates and going through the line of people filling their plates with food. I waited for a few people to go and meanwhile, different people I knew came to talk about their problems with me. I stood and listened to them. Finally, when my opportunity came for food, most of it was already gone. There were a few scrapings but not enough for a meal. A lady passed by and saw my predicament. She handed me a soup bowl and a bread and butter plate with food in them. I found an empty spot at one table. I set my dishes down and went in search of a chair. When I found a chair and came back, my dishes and food were gone. Were they stolen or removed? I was not sure. I felt horrible and resolved to deal with the hunger. After a while, I got up from my spot to see if there would be any food at all. To my surprise, I found a new stack of large, glass dinner plates. As I glanced in the distance, new food dishes began to appear. They were more appealing and beautifully decorated than the original ones. They were ornate and masterfully prepared. I had every opportunity to fill my plate with unbelievable, endless varieties of food. I was amazed and overjoyed. I had been truly blessed. Words cannot describe how delectable and appealing the varieties had become. Would this dream predict a revitalization of my intent for church involvement?

Sharla and I had planned a five-day getaway to Las Vegas during the past summer. We realized as we were sitting on the deck that we had never gone on a girl/mother/daughter holiday. We felt that January would be a good time for us to get away. It would be our winter escape. We planned to see a few shows and soon arranged all our bookings. One evening while Sharla and I were relaxing in our Las Vegas hotel room, I got an email saying that the lady who I knew from teaching had died unexpectedly that weekend. When the email totally registered in my memory, I realized that the prediction had come true. At first, it felt distant and not real. Soon, it impacted my whole being as the day replayed completely in my mind. The chances of the prediction happening were extremely remote. The lady was younger than me and healthy when I talked to her for the last time. I had promised God that I would erase doubt about His wishes for me. I was working on this book already. The sad new event would be another part that tied in with my strange knowledge. The book may not lead anywhere and I could be wasting my time. Terry assured me that the writing is therapeutic. I know that there is a reason for this book but just don't know what it is.

Lori and I began our bible study based on Sr. Miriam's book, "Loved as I Am" in February. The bible study ran for six weeks and was very wonderful and successful. We created it ourselves. Lori and I had prepared the sessions using Sr. Miriam's content. I had done a great deal of research and learning to be prepared. The learning was refreshing and I knew that I needed to continue with it. The bible study was held all of February until the middle of March. On March 24th was the last session. Deacon Joe did the reflection and VISION did the music. The participants noted how fortunate they were to have such a fantastic finish to the classes. There was now a good chance that Lori and I would be asked to repeat the bible study the following winter. I knew that I would gladly do it. Maybe, God is leading me to more learning and participation beyond this book. I still feel that the book that I am writing is meant to lead to something greater. Again, I need God to show me that path.

From Christmas to Easter, I was offered a part-time contract teaching in a grade three and four split classroom. One afternoon after I had arrived in the classroom but hadn't started teaching yet, Sr. Anna stopped by to visit. She displayed her big, beautiful smile and had a look of mischief in her eyes. Stopping close to me, she mentioned that she would be hosting a pilgrimage to Europe in October. She wished to know if I would be interested in traveling with her group. I loved the idea immediately and wondered if it would be practical. She noted that it was quite pricey but would be very worth it. That evening, I brought the brochure home to Terry and told him how much I wanted to go. He understood my desire and realized that this would give us an opportunity to see parts of Europe. We would probably never make a trip like this otherwise. I told Sr. Anna, "yes" that we would like to join her pilgrimage group. We would be visiting places like Lourdes and Fatima. I could hardly wait to see what it feels like to know that the Blessed Virgin Mary actually appeared in these places.

Now that the lady has passed away, it is really bothering me deep inside. I had inadvertently made a promise to God. It hurts when I think about it, even though I try hard not to. I don't understand the deep meaning of what had just happened. After Easter, I desperately needed to discuss this with a priest. No other person could possibly help me. Quite often I tried to tell myself that it wasn't real. I can't move past the deep emotion that I still struggled with. It was much too moving and real. It was a day that I actually lived through. The memory would not fade. It was a real tragedy that had happened. Even though I had no intention to continue discussing my unusual occurrences, I couldn't move past this one and needed to arrange time to speak with Father Steve again. I was hoping that the writing of this book would allow a new outlet for what was happening in my world instead. God seemed to pull me in a direction of His own intent and the tugging wouldn't disappear unless I followed it. I have learned from the past that the intense push doesn't relax unless I do what it asks of me. When I was at an evening Mass, I asked Father if I could talk to him after the busy Easter season was complete at church. He said that it would be good. Because I had already related the story twice to Terry, I wanted him to hear what Father had to say. I asked Terry to come with me. He has now come to be my true support. I can't help but remember how Terry and I now speak about my messages openly where as a year earlier; I was trying to convince him that they were real. I also believe that Father Steve may believe me now. He was the first person that the Holy Spirit sent me to for accountability. Following the meeting, I began to feel that my actions had been appropriate. I needed the reassurance that only someone with strong faith and knowledge could provide. Father was very easy to talk to and my own fears had put me through most of the sad experiences. Fear should not prevent God's messages from becoming known to all people even though it would be simple for me to keep them inside. The surprise of when they happen can't be described in words. The feeling is unique.

Substitute teaching has been back in my life for a year now and I really love doing it. Many of my assignments are back at the school that I retired from. The difference is that now I am not dealing with the daily stress and routines. I still have the love and respect of most students. A special day last year was one in which the priests were at the school for Reconciliation. I was teaching in the grade three/four and grade four classrooms. The principal came to the door and asked which of the students wished to receive the sacrament. Only a couple got out of their desks and lined up. It was very disappointing to see. I glanced around with a seriously sad look. One of the girls looked straight at me and asked, "Did you go to Reconciliation, Mrs. Schiissler?" I smiled at her and remembered receiving the sacrament the preceding week. I honestly could say, "Yes, I have." Immediately, half the class got out of their desks and joined the line. What a beautiful, subtle miracle I experienced that day that bears witness to my impact on these children.

Presently, I am experiencing a return to my Resurrection church community. Is it happening just like in the banquet dream? I joined the Spiritual Development committee and feel that it was a fantastic direction to move in. The committee can use the skills that I learned from my teaching career and it feels like a perfect fit. I love to plan and organize events for families and will be doing that for church activities. I love to teach and guide discussion. The new bible study, "James" allows me to do that as well. I feel renewed growth beginning.

During the months of May and June, Terry and I vacationed on Vancouver Island. Simple, meaningful messages are still occurring constantly in my life. Not all of them have great significance but some are truly notable. The last morning as we were leaving our cottage at the resort, I awakened from a dream. It told me that I was being requested to do something that my past learned skills would be needed for. That same day, I got a phone call on the ferryboat return to Vancouver telling me about my aunt passing away. Terry and I were asked to do readings at her funeral in Yorkton. The Saturday upon returning home I had already decided that I wanted to become involved in the Lay Ministry program. The church bulletin had instructions about informing your pastor for admission. Once again, I woke up that morning with the information that our pastor would be standing at the church door when I arrived. I would be wise to mention my wishes at that time. Confidently, I walked in the church and my knowledge was correct. Father was standing at the door. I followed the unexplainable instructions which couldn't help but make a person marvel at what just happened. While praying a couple of weeks later, the Holy Spirit informed me that it would be a good time to tell my daughter, Sharla about all my spiritual secrets that I had been keeping from her. Another unbelievable, beautiful surprise happened when she was receptive this time instead of negative as she often appeared in the past.

I worked on the drafting of this book for over a year, reliving all the events. It is strange how many of them have occurred and will never be forgotten. Call it coincidence or just luck, if you will. I have always felt a connection with God. God is real and interacts with us, I firmly believe. What I always found hard to believe is that He knows me among all people. I feel Him around me very often and can never dispute that. God may want more of me than just experiencing events that happened and letting them stay with me. My faith is now leading me to believe that I am intended to pass on all the things that God has done for me. I could never deny any of them because they are real. I lived all of them. God is speaking uniquely to me at the moment for some reason, I believe, and is not finished. He may want me to voice His mysteries and great works in my life. I also believe that God speaks to us every day and I am extremely happy that I talked to Him all these years. It is phenomenal and I feel blessed. Whatever God has to say to me next, I know that I am willing to listen. Most of the time, He places me out of my comfort zone. A couple of years ago, I would never have told my messages to anybody, except maybe Terry and my family. Now, I am willing to write about them in a book for everybody to read. My family will no longer be private, but public knowledge. Without speaking to Father Steve first, I wouldn't have had the courage to talk about "God in My Life" to any other person. Only God could have moved me in that direction and known how it would work.

The last chapter finalizes the events and messages for now. It is significant because Sr. Anna inspired both Terry and I to journey with her on a pilgrimage. The experience was entirely new to us and one that we would have never anticipated. The Holy Spirit was completely creating this time for both of us and we had no idea of what to expect. The impact had to be monumental because these are actual places where the Blessed Virgin Mary appeared to people. I wrote in a journal as the pilgrimage unfolded and hoped to feel where my messages may lead. Maybe there won't be messages because they only happen when God allows them and I have no way of knowing.

CHAPTER 16:

an account of my pilgrimage to europe

The pilgrimage was now getting near. There was only one week left until departure. The Sunday before that date had been set aside by Sister Anna for us to gather at Holy Child Church. She had arranged for a Pilgrim's blessing by Father Dan at the end of Mass. It was wonderful to be in the church again because many of the students that I had taught over the years were present. After the Mass, we met in a room for some food and last minute questions. I honestly admit that both Terry and I had fear about the trip since we had never flown this far from home before. I began to feel anxiety, even though I kept trying to tell myself that the trip is not a big deal. People fly all over world all the time and nothing generally goes wrong. Inside my mind, I kept feeling the horror of what people must experience when they know that their plane is accidentally going down. In the evening, Terry was playing for Mass at Holy Cross with "Joyful Noise", and instead of feeling happy, I began to experience panic. I thought that the upcoming week was going to be dreadful, fearing the day of departure. Instead of happiness and excitement, I was full of dread. As we left for church, I was beginning to feel ill with the stomach aches that I usually experience from uncertainty.

Sunday night before going to sleep, I said my prayers like I usually do. I asked God to give me strength to feel the joy of visiting such amazing places. I wanted to relax with the nearness of these divine locations and not waste my time wishing I was back home, thinking that something dreadful may happen. I woke up on Monday morning and the tiny, blue light was flashing on my cell phone. I checked for my emails, and especially the daily 3-Minute Retreat one. As I tapped on the entry, the first words that appeared on the screen were, "Do Not Be Afraid." Confidence replaced the apprehension I had just been feeling. What a wonderful beginning to my final week of home preparation and packing.

Many of our friends and acquaintances were tracking our departure date for the pilgrimage. Kind wishes were being sent our way. It was truly an event to anticipate. I felt relaxed and assured by how the fear almost dissipated entirely. The fear never really returned. Participants in the "James" study group commented that they felt God had a purpose for me to travel to Fatima and Lourdes. It was His will that the trip should take place. I believed what they told me. Burgos and Barcelona Spain were hardly mentioned at all in the conversations and Burgos was not a place that I knew anything about.

Friday evening was the beginning of my Lay Ministry training. The weekend would be spent at the Lumsden Retreat house. It would be a new experience. Everyone was very welcoming and I saw several familiar faces from our parish. The leaders were already informed that I was returning to Regina on Saturday afternoon instead of Sunday. The short Lay Ministry welcome was very rewarding. I would have loved to stay for the complete weekend program. The people kindly wished me their thoughts and prayers in the upcoming week. I even got some hugs from people I only met the previous day. I attended Saturday Mass back at Resurrection Church in Regina only to receive more well wishes for the upcoming pilgrimage. It was truly meant to be.

Sunday morning arrived much too soon. Contrary to earlier fears, there was no reason to fret over the airplane flight. It was comforting to travel with sixteen other pilgrims. Immediately seeing Sister Anna at the airport made me feel that everything would be well. The other people in our group were very social, warm, and friendly. It was evident that we would all get along and have a fantastic tour together. After many hours of flying, there was concern over rough turbulence between Frankfurt, Germany and Lisbon, Portugal. Some people admitted that they were praying as the plane rocked and felt that it may break apart from all the tossing and jarring movement. I kept thinking, "Do not be afraid", and I wasn't afraid at that time or at any other time during the pilgrimage. Around lunch time, we arrived at Lisbon as scheduled and with our baggage in hand.

By Monday afternoon, we were settled in the Hotel Fatima. There we met a great new group of pilgrims from Alameda, California, lead by Father Joy, who were to accompany us on our journey. Fatima was beautiful but the weather was rainy. After a dinner of local food, Terry and I walked across the Sanctuary to an outdoor, partly enclosed chapel. We were mostly amazed at the large size of the Sanctuary. It was easily larger than three football fields. There were various buildings, including a newly constructed church that could hold thousands of people at one time. We toured the church but were not scheduled to have Mass in it. In the evening, we attended a candlelight procession. We were warned to arrive early to obtain a possible seat for the liturgy. Even though the wind was brisk and strong, along with rain pelting us, we were in the company of thousands of people. They were crowded into the small space. We all moved closer together as more people kept joining in the group to celebrate. Everyone was quietly speaking with reverence at the beginning and then quieted as the proceedings began. We learned that we were in the Chapel of the Apparitions which housed the small chapel that the Blessed Virgin Mary asked the children to have built. When the priest began to pray candles were lit, just like at an Easter Vigil. People passed on the fire to each other with a flowing display being created. The beauty was felt in the sharing as strange people of all nationalities cooperated in lighting each other's candles. "Thank you", was expressed in many different languages when the wind blew out the candles and they needed to be relit many times. As the procession was about to begin, it started to rain harder. The crowd was not deterred. They used umbrellas or just raincoats to protect themselves. The people processed around the huge square in the pouring rain, while an enormous statue of the Blessed Virgin Mary was being carried in the lead. The praying and gathering of people was very inspirational.

Tuesday morning was scheduled to tour Fatima. We departed by coach to Aljustrel where the three children who witnessed the apparition of the Blessed Virgin Mary were born. Descending from the bus instantly created a feeling of being overwhelmed. It felt like the song, and I was now standing on "Holy Ground". Big tears started falling on their own without any feeling of sadness – just unbelievable joy. Walking along stone-lined streets which still exist, makes a person feel like they are back in time. You get a strong impression that something unbelievable happened here.

We returned to the coach and continued on to Santarem to see the shrine of the Most Holy Miracle (a Eucharistic miracle). Back in Fatima, Father Joy, our pilgrimage traveling priest, said Mass for us in a simple chapel, he was assisted by resident priests.

Wednesday morning we departed Fatima for Burgos, Spain. The full day drive would have seemed long without the planned activities. Once on the road we did the Morning Prayer and later prayed the rosary. We were so fortunate to be traveling with a sister and a priest to lead us. The tour guide was interesting because he was very knowledgeable about the history of the regions we were visiting. As the day progressed we stopped for lunch. After returning to the coach the movie, "The Way" was shown on the upper screens. Strangely, it was depicting a pilgrimage of Camino de Santiago which is filmed in Burgos, Spain, exactly where we were headed.

After checking into our hotel, we walked across the center town plaza to the basilica. A side chapel was available for our group to have Mass. Father Joy was our Presider and Sr. Anna arranged the songs and readings. She asked me to do the reading. I was honoured to have an opportunity to proclaim in such an ornate location. It was definitely a once in a lifetime experience. After a late dinner, we returned to our room for a good night sleep.

The pilgrimage was passing by much too quickly. It was soon Thursday morning and we met for a guided tour of the basilica. The "Catedral de Burgos", which is dedicated to the Virgin Mary, tour began. The tour guide provided detailed, extremely interesting information about the Gothic architecture. Strangely, I kept hearing the name James repeated many times. Closer listening taught me that it was the same St. James of whom I'm doing the bible study. I hadn't researched him to any extent. Yet, I was learning about him for two days now. Outdoors, I witnessed young people with backpacks continuing on their pilgrimage which would end at the shrine of the apostle St. James the Great in the Cathedral of Santiago de Compostela in Galacia, Northwestern Spain. The route is approximately 500 miles or 800 kilometers long. Burgos is about the half way point of the pilgrimage.

St. James became a martyr by beheading in Jerusalem 44 AD. He spent time preaching the gospel in Spain, but returned to Judea after seeing a vision of the Virgin Mary on the bank of the Ebros River. After his death, his disciples shipped his body to the Iberian Peninsula (Spain) to be buried in Santiago, off the coast of Spain. A heavy storm hit the ship and the body was lost in the ocean. After some time it washed ashore undamaged and covered in scallops. The shell grooves of the scallops meet at a single point representing the many routes which arrive at a single destination. The shell is a metaphor for the pilgrims. God's hands guide the pilgrims just like they guided St. James to shore. The shells symbolize the pilgrims that walk plus they mark the route to take on the pilgrimage journey.

I can't help but question why I traveled on a pilgrimage to Spain that lines me up with pilgrims of St. James. Without Sister Anna asking me to join her, I would have never taken this journey. Without randomly choosing James as my bible study, the pilgrimage route of Burgos would never have meant the same. Feelings of unbelievable surprise surface about the strange coincidence of what is now happening.

Evening Mass at the chapel was meaningful once again. Dinner was lamb chops upstairs in a quaint little restaurant. Burgos was a fantastic city and possibly a favourite one.

Friday morning we began traveling through Northern Spain, into Basque country. We made a couple of stops and eventually arrived in Lourdes, France. This is the home of St. Bernadette Soubirous. She witnessed the apparition of the Blessed Virgin Mary in a grotto. After many visits, she was asked to dig into the ground to uncover a spring of water. While she was digging and people were watching her, they witnessed only some mud. Bernadette covered her face and upper body with the mud. The people watching thought she was mad and left the area to return home. When they had just left, a spring poured out of the ground in that exact spot to form a pool. The water demonstrated healing powers, first to her father who had blindness in an eye, and later to the many thousands of people who pilgrimage to the healing water. People still continue to come to the healing waters to this very day.

We toured the church where St. Bernadette was baptized. Only the baptismal font remains from the original church which burned down many years ago. We visited the hospital where she was born. Later it became the paternal house. St. Bernadette's family became very poor when her father lost his job as a miller. They lived in an old vacant part of a prison for a while. We saw the home they later resided in. A similar affect fell upon me as happened a year earlier with Saint Brother Andre. There was a large picture of St. Bernadette and I could see her eyes staring at me with a piercing look. They seemed to be following me as I walked by. I felt very uncomfortable and challenged. What is she trying to tell me? The evening procession was bypassed because Terry and I both felt very tired.

Saturday morning at 6:45a.m.our group of pilgrims, met at the grotto in Lourdes, France for Mass. The Mass was presided over by the bishop. It was dark and very cold. In spite of the weather, the sanctuary was already crowded with people. We could see people coming and going in all different directions despite the hour. There were many religious orders represented as a person would glance around. Once again we got to celebrate Mass with Father Joy assisting this time. Returning to the Alba hotel improved our spirits when we warmed up and ate some breakfast. Later in the morning, we returned to fetch some water from the Lourdes spigot at the grotto. There was an immense feeling of reverence as the vast numbers of people were observed participating in the ongoing activities by either kneeling, sitting, or standing with their voices chanting in prayer. Reconciliation is offered almost continuously in trailers with a few rooms at the outer areas of the sanctuary. We spent the remainder of time souvenir shopping at the dozens of Catholic religious gift shops.

After lunch we had the opportunity to walk the Way of the Cross. The pathway was very steep as it ascended one of the Pyrenees Mountains. It took us an hour to climb and brake along the rugged, stony trail. The stations were carved out of a wood like, brown material and were immense in size. We were an exhausted, small group of pilgrims lead by Father Joy. I loved how Father's name definitely suited him with his warm, ever-present smile. Another fantastic dinner meal ended the day.

Sunday was the only day without Mass but we had celebrated it on Saturday night. We drove all day by motor coach. Morning Prayer was said along the way just as it was every morning that we traveled. The only stop was at Carcassone which is a medieval town with a castle, fortress, and double walls. It is a very unique experience for a Canadian.

Our last full day on the pilgrimage had now arrived. Terry and I decided to remain in Barcelona and do some sightseeing there on our own. Other pilgrims from our group went to Montserrat, a Benedictine monastery, but since my ankle was still swollen from the original flight and continued walking, I did not wish to climb any more mountains. The whole pilgrim group met at the hotel after their return in the afternoon. It would be our final time together before everyone leaves for home tomorrow.

The group boarded the coach and we were given a tour of the city of Barcelona. Afterwards, arrangements had been made for tickets to the Sagrada Familia. We had Mass in the crypt of Antonio Gaudi, the renowned architect. Unfortunately, the basilica does not allow Mass to be celebrated for the people in the main chapel. The belief is that they will have an opportunity to see the inside without having to pay. The focus is to raise large amounts of money for the completion of this immense, Gothic structure. I felt disappointed upon leaving because churches should always be available for the people. No person should be refrained from entering a church because of a lack of money. The evening concluded with a fine restaurant supper followed by a cup of melted heavy chocolate and deep fried doughnuts, called churros. We just had to try them in spite of the many calories.

As a quick moment presented itself at the end of the pilgrimage, I was given an opportunity to reflect. I could now feel the good fortune of my life so far. The blessings God has given me can not be counted. The little girl that played in a corner of our farm yard would have never envisioned what would come to her because she always believed in God. Sitting in a soft chair at a downtown Barcelona hotel, feels far removed from Melville, Saskatchewan. When I was eighteen years old and given a knowing about the possible future pains to come, it destroyed the strong love that I had for the Blessed Mother at that time. When my first baby died, I blamed her for not caring about me. I couldn't forgive her and felt that she could have asked God to prevent it from happening. I never seriously prayed to the Blessed Virgin Mary and always focused on Jesus.

After the many pilgrimage hours I had just experienced, I felt the devotion to Mary by the thousands of people, and have truly asked for forgiveness. I will let that part of my life go. God gave me renewed love and respect for His mother. I could never leave the pilgrimage and not be changed forever. As I gazed up at the many places that she appeared, I knew that she is truly amazing and special to be the Mother of God.

I have now reached a good stopping point in my book. I can hear the bells of the basilica. God really did put me here to educate me. Now, it is my mission once again to return home and continue in His plan for me. God please grant me the wisdom and the grace to do your will.

While flying home from Barcelona on Tuesday morning, I was tired and ecstatic about my awesome experience. I looked around and thoughts of how all the other traveling partners were sitting together while Terry and I had been separated and placed beside strangers couldn't help but surface. Every flight had us separated and I felt it wasn't fair. Having hour upon hour to think about the dilemma, lead me to believe that the only possible outcome could be anger and disappointment. All the love of God and recent experience could have been in vain. It would be so simple to let all the love and learning disappear in a bad moment. I had to move past this time and use it to teach me about what I had just experienced. I have to move my thoughts to how God has just spoiled me with His love. No matter what effort I pursue, I can never repay what He has allowed in my life. I can only continue to love Him more and more, while letting those terrible feelings and the many more negative feelings that will still continue to come, go before they become rooted.

As I begin to tell others about my book, they are beginning to tell me about their spiritual experiences. There is new discussion about God's many gifts openly offered into my knowledge. I am feeling how God's deeds are being witnessed and now being shared because I openly started speaking about "God in My Life". I now pray to share my faith more openly like the many people in Portugal, Spain, and France. I want to become less reserved about my faith and beliefs and more open in sharing how wonderful our God is. I know that He continues to have more surprises in store for me.

EPILOGUE

The memory of beginning to write this nonfiction account of my spiritual events can only be described as an afternoon of fear and frustration. I could not believe that I was committing myself to months of reliving many painful family events that I had worked hard to bury in the past. At first, I didn't think that I would even move beyond the first chapter. In fact, I rewrote the first chapter three times before I felt that it even could be read by someone and make sense. Slowly but surely, the next few chapters began to flow. Eventually, I couldn't stop writing. I felt full of the Holy Spirit and knew that the later chapters were telling of how God had worked in my life from the beginning to the present. There was an indescribable sequence of events showing God's hands at work continuously influencing everything that happened.

A year later, I still couldn't move past attempting to perfect what I was trying to say. How can you impress on people the way that God works in our lives on a daily basis? It was "you must see it to believe it" knowledge that things happened in reality. Others probably would not see it from that particular perspective. I began to debate whether this spiritual account was meant to be published or not. It would be easy to delete it as not ever having happened and not have to share my personal history with others. I realized that self-publishing would be expensive and I debated whether all future substitute teaching income should be used as payment for the publishing of this book, instead of for fun and travel. I had only worked for three half days in November and asked God for a sign whether to proceed with publishing or not. In early December, after my request, the next day I received a personal cheque for income tax money that I was not aware of being owed. That week, I was called for more days of work than I was expecting. My revenue for the publication of this book began to grow. I asked other people who I had shared my story with whether they thought the events were a coincidence or a sign from God. I was assured by everyone that it was a sign from God and I must do what I had promised Him.

Dedicated to everyone who recognizes God's
love and shares it with others.

AND

Especially, the people named in the book who
allowed me to reveal their role in my life.

PATRICIA SHIISSLER | AUTHOR

SHARLA WEBSTER | ILLUSTRATOR

CPSIA information can be obtained
at www.ICGtesting.com
Printed in the USA
LVOW12s0904280318
571443LV00001B/65/P